Entering the Dragon's Lair

Chinese Antiaccess Strategies and Their Implications for the United States

Roger Cliff · Mark Burles · Michael S. Chase · Derek Eaton · Kevin L. Pollpeter

Prepared for the United States Air Force

RAND PROJECT AIR FORCE

The research described in this report was sponsored by the United States Air Force under Contracts FA7014-06-C-0001 and F49642-01-C-0003. Further information may be obtained from the Strategic Planning Division, Directorate of Plans, Hq USAF.

Library of Congress Cataloging-in-Publication Data

Entering the dragon's lair : Chinese antiaccess strategies and their implications for the United States / Roger Cliff ... [et al.].
    p. cm.
    Includes bibliographical references.
    ISBN 978-0-8330-3995-8 (pbk. : alk. paper)
    1. Military doctrine—China. 2. China—Military policy—21st century. 3. United States—Military policy—21st century. I. Cliff, Roger.

UA835.E41 2007
355'.033551—dc22

2007007157

Published 2007 by the RAND Corporation
1776 Main Street, P.O. Box 2138, Santa Monica, CA 90407-2138
1200 South Hayes Street, Arlington, VA 22202-5050
4570 Fifth Avenue, Suite 600, Pittsburgh, PA 15213-2665
RAND URL: http://www.rand.org/
To order RAND documents or to obtain additional information, contact
Distribution Services: Telephone: (310) 451-7002;
Fax: (310) 451-6915; Email: order@rand.org

Preface

U.S. defense analysts have become concerned in recent years about the possibility of a U.S. adversary employing an "antiaccess" strategy—actions that would impede the deployment of U.S. forces into the combat theater, limit the locations from which those forces could effectively operate, or force them to operate from locations farther from the locus of conflict than they would normally prefer. China is often proposed as a potential adversary that could employ such a strategy. To date, however, there has been no published comprehensive assessment of what specific types of antiaccess methods Chinese military strategists are contemplating and that China might attempt to employ in a conflict with the United States.

This report is the result of a project on "Chinese Antiaccess Concepts and Capabilities," whose purpose was to determine what types of antiaccess measures China might employ in the event of a conflict with the United States, assess the potential effects of such measures, and identify actions the United States can take and capabilities it should acquire to reduce these effects.

The research reported here was conducted within the RAND Project AIR FORCE Strategy and Doctrine Program and was sponsored by the Air Force Deputy Chief of Staff for Air and Space Operations (AF/XO) and the Commander, Pacific Air Forces (PACAF/CC) and conducted within the Strategy and Doctrine.

It is part of an ongoing effort by Project AIR FORCE to assess the nature and implications of the growth in Chinese military power. Previous publications from this effort include the following:

- Evan S. Medeiros, Roger Cliff, Keith Crane, and James C. Mulvenon, *A New Direction for China's Defense Industry*, MG-334-AF, 2005.
- Keith Crane, Roger Cliff, Evan Medeiros, James C. Mulvenon, and William Overholt, *Modernizing China's Military: Opportunities and Constraints*, MG-260-1-AF, 2005.
- Kevin Pollpeter, *U.S.-China Security Management: Assessing the Military-to-Military Relationship*, MG-143-AF, 2004.
- Zalmay Khalilzad, David T. Orletsky, Jonathan Pollack, Kevin Pollpeter, Angel M. Rabasa, David A. Shlapak, Abram N. Shulsky, and Ashley J. Tellis, *The United States and Asia: Toward a New U.S. Strategy and Force Posture*, MR-1315-AF, 2001.
- Roger Cliff, *The Military Potential of China's Commercial Technology*, MR-1292-AF, 2001.
- Erica Strecker Downs, *China's Quest for Energy Security*, MR-1244-AF, 2000.
- Richard Sokolsky, Angel Rabasa, and C.R. Neu, *The Role of Southeast Asia in U.S. Strategy Toward China*, MR-1170-AF, 2000.
- Abram N. Shulsky, *Deterrence Theory and Chinese Behavior*, MR-1161-AF, 2000.
- Mark Burles and Abram N. Shulsky, *Patterns in China's Use of Force: Evidence from History and Doctrinal Writings*, MR-1160-AF, 2000.
- Michael D. Swaine and Ashley J. Tellis, *Interpreting China's Grand Strategy: Past, Present, and Future*, MR-1121-AF, 2000.
- Daniel L. Byman and Roger Cliff, *China's Arms Sales: Motivations and Implications*, MR-1119-AF, 1999.
- Zalmay Khalilzad, Abram N. Shulsky, Daniel Byman, Roger Cliff, David T. Orletsky, David A. Shlapak, and Ashley J. Tellis, *The United States and a Rising China: Strategic and Military Implications*, MR-1082-AF, 1999.
- Mark Burles, *Chinese Policy Toward Russia and the Central Asian Republics*, MR-1045-AF, 1999.

The information in this report is current as of June 2006.

RAND Project AIR FORCE

RAND Project AIR FORCE (PAF), a division of the RAND Corporation, is the U.S. Air Force's federally funded research and development center for studies and analyses. PAF provides the Air Force with independent analyses of policy alternatives affecting the development, employment, combat readiness, and support of current and future aerospace forces. Research is conducted in four programs: Aerospace Force Development; Manpower, Personnel, and Training; Resource Management; and Strategy and Doctrine.

Additional information about PAF is available on our Web site at http://www.rand.org/paf.

Contents

Figures

Summary

Since the end of the Cold War, U.S. strategists have become increasingly concerned with the possibility that, in the event of a conflict with the United States, an adversary might adopt and attempt to execute an "antiaccess" strategy intended to interfere with the U.S. military's ability to deploy to or operate within overseas theaters of operation. This concern stems from two features of the post–Cold War world. First is that, with the disintegration of the Soviet Union, no country fields military forces comparable in both quantity and quality to those of the United States, and thus there is little likelihood that the U.S. military will be defeated in a conventional force-on-force engagement on the battlefield. The principal threat to defeat U.S. military forces, therefore, is through the use of an asymmetric approach, such as an antiaccess strategy.

The chances of success of an antiaccess strategy are increased by the second feature of the post–Cold War world: The absence of a single dominant adversary makes it impossible to predict where U.S. military forces will next be needed and, thus, makes it likely that the United States will have relatively few forward-deployed forces in the vicinity of a conflict about to erupt.

For potential opponents of the United States, the motives for adopting an antiaccess strategy are compelling. These countries must plan to face an adversary that enjoys tremendous military and technological superiority, and they undoubtedly recognize that, as long as the U.S. military can arrive in force and on time, it will almost certainly prevail. Thus, they may seek to impede the deployment of U.S. forces and restrict or disrupt the U.S. military's ability to operate within a theater far from U.S. territory. They may also calculate that, by mounting a credible threat to do so, they will be able to deter the United States from intervening in the first place, or at least limit the scale and scope of that intervention.

This monograph describes the types of antiaccess measures one particular country—China—might employ in a future conflict with the United States, how these measures might affect U.S. military operations in the event of a conflict between the United States and China, and possible ways the United States can reduce the effects of these measures. For purposes of this discussion, an *antiaccess* measure is considered to be any action by an opponent that has the effect of slowing the deployment of friendly forces into a theater, preventing them from operating from certain locations within that theater, or causing them to operate from distances farther from the locus of conflict than they would normally prefer. Potential Chinese actions that could affect U.S. access to areas around China were identified through the analysis of Chinese military doctrinal writings. These included books on military doctrine, articles from Chinese military journals, reports from Chinese military newspapers, and recent Western studies of Chinese strategic thinking. The potential effects of Chinese antiaccess measures were assessed by examining the capability of the Chinese military to actually implement these measures and by analyzing how such implementation would affect U.S. military operations. Possible U.S. measures to reduce the effects of these measures were identified by consulting with RAND Corporation and external experts on the associated areas of military operations.

The possibility that the Chinese People's Liberation Army (PLA) might employ antiaccess measures in a conflict with the United States is the product of the PLA's view of the nature of modern war, its awareness of China's military weaknesses, and its recognition of U.S. military superiority. Because of the rise of important political and economic centers in China's coastal regions, China's military strategy has shifted from defending the continent to defending areas on China's periphery and maritime force projection. Instead of fighting a "People's War" involving human-wave attacks, the PLA is now preparing to fight a "local war under high-technology conditions." PLA strategists expect such conflicts to be characterized by limited political objectives and the use of information technology and by being highly mobile, lethal, and resource intensive. (See pp. 18–23.)

Chinese writers are keenly aware that the PLA, despite the considerable progress it has made in recent years, still lags behind the U.S. military in terms of technology, doctrine, training, and experience and that any conflict against the U.S. military will pose extreme challenges. To defeat a technologically superior enemy, such as the United States, the PLA has focused on devising strategies that maximize China's relative strengths and that create opportunities to exploit adversary weaknesses. Consequently, the PLA would not seek to confront the U.S. military in a force-on-force battle but instead would seek to strike decisively at U.S. vulnerabilities. In addition, the PLA views seizing the initiative at the outset of a conflict as imperative to defeating a technologically superior opponent. As a result, Chinese writings emphasize "gaining mastery by striking first," possibly through surprise attack or preemption. This suggests that Chinese leaders might consider preemptively attacking U.S. forces as they are deploying to a region in what U.S. policymakers intend as an action to *deter* a conflict. (See pp. 23–44.)

PLA writings have identified several perceived strategic U.S. vulnerabilities. First is the possibility that U.S. forces could be involved in two major contingency operations simultaneously. PLA writers have observed that even a relatively limited engagement, like the 1999 conflict with Serbia over Kosovo, requires significant U.S. forces and that timing a military operation for when the United States was already engaged could mean that the United States would not have enough forces available to respond to China's actions. In addition, some Chinese strategists calculate that the perceived U.S. aversion to casualties might be exploited by delivering a sudden blow aimed at causing a large number of U.S. military casualties, sowing doubt and discontent among the U.S. population, and potentially forcing the withdrawal of U.S. forces. Most significantly for this study, some Chinese analysts have suggested that the dependence of the United States on potentially unreliable friends and allies for access to forward bases and support presents opportunities for China to pressure these countries to limit or deny the United States use of these facilities. (See pp. 44–50.)

Although the Chinese military doctrinal writings we examined for this study do not explicitly discuss antiaccess as a separate and distinct strategy, they do suggest that Chinese doctrine for defeating a militarily superior adversary, such as the United States, includes a number of tactics that are clearly antiaccess in intention or effect. The PLA has identified the U.S. military's reliance on information systems as a significant vulnerability that, if successfully exploited, could paralyze or degrade U.S. forces to such an extent that victory could be achieved. In particular, PLA analysts believe that attacks against information systems can delay the deployment of U.S. military forces by disrupting communications or denying the U.S. military access to information on enemy whereabouts. PLA analysts note that information warfare can employ either "soft-kill" and "hard-kill" methods. Soft-kill methods include computer network attacks and electronic jamming, while possible hard-kill methods include directed energy weapons, explosives, and kinetic energy attacks. Targets could include computer systems based in the United States or abroad, command and control nodes, and space-based intelligence, surveillance, and reconnaissance and communications assets. (See pp. 51–60.)

Noting the great distances that U.S. forces would need to travel in a conflict with China, attacks against logistic systems are also discussed. The goals of these attacks would be to delay the deployment of additional U.S. forces to the region and to render existing forces in the region less effective or more vulnerable by preventing timely supplies of the materiel needed for warfighting. Attacks against logistic systems described in PLA writings include blockades, attacking supply depots, and striking at air or sea supply missions. (See pp. 60–62.)

PLA writings also discuss attacks against air bases and ports. Such attacks would prevent or disrupt the inflow of personnel and supplies, as well as the basing of air and naval assets. PLA analysts state that attacking these targets is the most efficient way to gain air or sea superiority, although the difficulty of achieving success is not understated. While no source specifically indicated which U.S. bases might be attacked, the importance that bases in the western Pacific would have for U.S. military operations in a conflict with China suggests that they may be key targets for PLA planners. (See pp. 62–71.)

Similarly, the importance of naval aviation to U.S. operations is of great concern to the PLA. Chinese sources describe the disproportionate role aircraft carriers sometimes play in conflict but also make clear their belief that aircraft carriers can be defeated. Massed attacks using air- and sea-launched cruise missiles can be used to overwhelm an aircraft carrier's defenses, and submarine-launched torpedoes can be used in ambush. Ballistic missiles are also discussed as possible anticarrier weapons. (See pp. 71–76.)

In addition to military strategies, China might also use diplomatic and political strategies to deny or limit the use of forward bases, most notably in Japan. While Chinese writings are not explicit in discussing strategies to limit or deny support to the United States, interviews with Chinese military officers suggest that deterrence and coercion, including threats of force, could be used against Japan. (See pp. 77–79.)

If China were to employ them as described above in a conflict with the United States, such measures could significantly disrupt U.S. military operations as a whole and specifically slow the deployment of U.S. forces to the theater of operations, prevent them from operating from certain locations within the theater of operations, and/or cause them to operate from distances greater than the U.S. military would otherwise prefer. In particular, Chinese antiaccess measures could severely degrade the ability of U.S. forces to operate from airfields near China; impede the deployment of forces to forward operating locations; degrade command and control, early warning, or supply capabilities for forward-deployed forces to the point that the theater commander would choose to withdraw them to more distant locations; and prevent naval surface assets from operating in waters near China. (See pp. 81–93.)

The net result of these effects could be that the United States would actually be defeated in a conflict with China—not in the sense that the U.S. military would be destroyed but in the sense that China would accomplish its military and political objectives while preventing the United States from accomplishing some or all of its political and military objectives. Moreover, even if Chinese antiaccess measures did not result in the outright defeat of the United States, they would likely make it significantly more costly for the United States to operate in the region, and these costs could even rise to the point at which the United States was unwilling to pay them. Finally, even if Chinese antiaccess strategies did not result in the United States being unwilling or unable to defeat China, Chinese decisionmakers might convince themselves that they *would* cause the United States to be unwilling or unable to intervene successfully. If the decisionmakers then chose to take actions that would cause China to come into conflict with the United States, the result would be a costly and bloody war that would not otherwise have occurred. (See pp. 111–114.)

The United States can, however, can take a number of actions to counter Chinese antiaccess threats, including the following:

- strengthening passive defenses at air bases
- deploying air and missile defense systems near critical facilities
- diversifying basing options for aircraft
- strengthening defenses against attacks by covert operatives (PLA special operations forces or covert agents under the control of China's nonmilitary intelligence services)
- reducing the vulnerability of naval forces to attack while in port
- reducing the vulnerability of command, control, communications, computer, intelligence, surveillance, and reconnaissance systems
- taking steps both to deter and to mitigate the potential effects of high-altitude nuclear detonations
- bolstering allied capabilities. (See pp. 95–103.)

Moreover, given the concern that Chinese decisionmakers could convince themselves that antiaccess tactics might cause the United States to be unwilling or unable to intervene successfully in a conflict, these actions should be openly publicized to reduce the likelihood that China might embark on actions that would result in a confrontation with the United States.

A number of new or improved capabilities would further enhance U.S. ability to counter Chinese antiaccess strategies, including the following:

- improved ballistic missile defenses
- a capability to detect, identify, and attack mobile, time-sensitive targets
- improved land-based and advanced shipborne cruise missile defenses
- improved antisubmarine warfare capabilities
- improved minesweeping capabilities
- an antisatellite capability, as well as counters to antisatellite attack
- an extended-range air defense capability
- counters to long-range surface-to-air and air-to-air missiles
- early strategic and tactical warning capabilities. (See pp. 103–109.)

The potential Chinese antiaccess threat is significant, but there is much the United States can do to mitigate the threat. Some of these measures are relatively low cost, but others will require additional capabilities, and still others may require a fundamental reassessment of operational doctrine and plans.

Acknowledgments

This report is the product of the efforts of many more people than those listed as authors. The authors would particularly like to thank the other participants in the study on which it is based: Michael Lostumbo, K. Scott McMahon, David Orletsky, Garret Albert, Nicholas Dienna, Michael Glosny, and Eric Valko. Although they did not directly author any sections of this report, they were integral members of the overall project, and their insights and suggestions are reflected throughout.

A number of analysts contributed their expertise to various portions of the study. Particularly important contributions were made by David Finkelstein of CNA Corporation and David Ochmanek of RAND, who reviewed another report from this same project; by Bruce Pirnie of RAND and a reviewer who asked not to be named, who reviewed an earlier version of this report; and by Robert Button of RAND who was not a formal reviewer of either report but who, entirely on his own initiative, read both closely, provided detailed comments on both, and provided extensive amounts of additional advice and consultation. John Gordon, Frank Lacroix, Roger Molander, Toy Reid, David Shlapak, and Carl Stephens of RAND and Lt Col Michael Gantt and Lt Col Gregory Marzolf of the U.S. Air Force also provided valuable advice and assistance. In addition, invaluable project support was provided by our liaisons at Headquarters, U.S. Air Force, Lt Col Marzolf and Maj Michael Pietrucha, as well as by the staff at Headquarters, Pacific Air Forces, particularly Lt Col David Dahl, Capt Matt Santoro, Maj Jim Sears, and Deric Wong.

Sarah Harting and Jane Siegel of RAND provided vital assistance in the production of the initial versions of this monograph; Olivia Contreras-Saenz supplied timely budgetary updates; and Maggie Mendez provided vital personnel assistance. Susan Junda of Dynamic Solutions provided superb instruction and follow-on support in project planning and management. Phyllis Gilmore of RAND provided efficient and extremely high-quality editing.

From conception to publication, this project has spanned the tenures of three directors or acting directors of PAF's Strategy and Doctrine Program: Edward Harshberger, Alan Vick, and Andrew Hoehn. The authors would like to thank all three, and the rest of PAF's management, for their support, encouragement, valuable critiques, patience, and understanding throughout this process.

Many other people not mentioned above also contributed to this project, and the authors apologize to anyone whose contribution was not acknowledged but should have been. The authors also take sole responsibility for any errors in this report.

Abbreviations

AAM	air-to-air missile
AMS	Academy of Military Sciences
ASCM	antiship cruise missile
ASW	antisubmarine warfare
AWACS	Airborne Warning and Control System
C^4ISR	command, control, communications, computers, intelligence, surveillance, and reconnaissance
CBRNE	chemical, biological, radiological, nuclear, enhanced high explosive
CEP	circular error probable
CONOPS	concept of operations
DoD	U.S. Department of Defense
DSB	Defense Science Board
EMP	electromagnetic pulse
FBIS	Foreign Broadcast Information Service
MEADS	Medium Extended Air Defense System
NATO	North Atlantic Treaty Organization
NDP	National Defense Panel

OSD	Office of the Secretary of Defense
PAC-3	Patriot Advanced Capability-3
PAF	RAND Project AIR FORCE
PLA	People's Liberation Army
PLAN	People's Liberation Army Navy
PRC	People's Republic of China
QDR	Quadrennial Defense Review
SAM	surface-to-air missile
SLAMRAAM	Surface-Launched Advanced Medium Range Air-to-Air Missile
SOF	special operations forces
WMD	weapons of mass destruction

Introduction

The concept of *antiaccess*—the idea that an opponent of the United States may seek to interfere actively with the U.S. military's ability to deploy to or operate within overseas theaters of operations—began to emerge as an important theme in U.S. strategic writings in the 1990s. Perhaps the earliest formulation of the idea was in a paper written by Andrew Krepinevich in 1992, while he worked at the Office of Net Assessment in the Pentagon. He stated that "many competitors . . . will probably have the . . . goal of information, space, sea, and air *denial*, as opposed to seeking control or domination" (Krepinevich, 2002, p. 44; emphasis in the original).[1] In its 1996 report on strategic mobility, the Defense Science Board (DSB), while also not expressly using the term *antiaccess*, noted that "future adversaries will have the motives and likely the means to seriously disrupt U.S. strategic deployments" by coercing other states into not cooperating with U.S. deployment efforts or by directly attacking ports and airfields; logistics nodes; strategic transport assets; and command, control, communications, and computer systems with missiles, mines, special operations forces (SOF), aircraft, submarines, offensive information warfare, weapons of mass destruction (WMD), or advanced conventional weapons (DSB, 1996, pp. 52–56).[2] This early characterization of the antiaccess problem is broadly reflected in most subsequent analyses of the issue.

---

[1] The quote is taken from the Center for Strategic and Budgetary Assessment's recent reissue of the paper.

[2] At about the same time, Chinese scholars noted that one way for a "weak" power to defeat a "high-technology" adversary was to launch a preemptive strike against that adversary while

The motives for adopting an antiaccess strategy are theoretically compelling: If the U.S. military can arrive in force, it will almost undoubtedly win in a conventional military campaign. A rational opponent should thus seek to acquire the capabilities necessary to disrupt or delay U.S. deployment activities or to deny it the use of regional bases in the hope that, by successfully doing so or threatening to do so, it will prevent or deter the United States from acting (DSB, 1996, p. 55).[3]

Denial of access cannot be considered a new strategic goal. After all, a major goal of German submarine operations in the North Atlantic after the entry of the United States into World War II was to prevent the deployment and supply of U.S. forces in Europe. Similarly, Germany's "Atlantic Wall" along the coast of France was intended to prevent Allied ground forces from being able to enter the northern European mainland theater of operations. During the Cold War, the United States put considerable military effort into ensuring that Russian submarines would not be able to interfere with the flow of U.S. ground forces across the Atlantic and into Western Europe. What has given the problem of antiaccess increased saliency in recent years is the disintegration of the Soviet Union and the associated uncertainty about where U.S. military forces will next be needed. During the Cold War, the United States focused on preventing a Soviet offensive against Western Europe and maintained substantial forces in that region to respond to such a possibility.[4] With the demise of the Soviet Union, there is no longer a single dominant threat against which forces can

---

it was deploying. Harbors, airports, and strategic airlift and sealift were all identified as desirable targets. In addition, the scholars stated that Iraq's passivity in the face of a U.S. military buildup played an important role in Iraq's defeat during the 1991 Gulf War. (See Lu Linzhi, 1996, p. 6, and Sun Zian, 1995, pp. 10–11.)

[3] In practice, however, the logic of a preemptive antiaccess strategy, particularly one using WMD, may be far less compelling if the possibility remains that the conflict might otherwise be avoided or contained. It is interesting to note that, in the winter of 2002–2003, Iraq took no antiaccess actions in the face of both a lengthy U.S. military buildup in the Gulf region and the near certainty of a conflict.

[4] As the reference above to the flow of U.S. ground forces across the Atlantic and into Western Europe suggests, of course, this does not mean that there could not have been an antiaccess problem even during the Cold War.

be forward deployed. Thus, wherever the next crisis erupts, the United States will have relatively fewer forward-deployed forces on hand than it would have had in the event of a Soviet invasion of Western Europe.[5] With fewer forward-deployed forces to defend U.S. strategic interests and to protect the bases necessary for the flow of reinforcements into a theater, it has become conceivable that a relatively weak power could adopt and execute a strategy that successfully interferes with the U.S. military's ability to project power.

The Antiaccess Challenge in Department of Defense Strategy and Policy Publications

The 1997 Quadrennial Defense Review (QDR) only tangentially reflected the concerns the DSB had raised, but the threat enemy antiaccess action poses has gained increasing prominence in U.S. Department of Defense (DoD) strategy and policy documents ever since.[6] The December 1997 National Defense Panel (NDP) report on transforming defense recognized antiaccess as a future operational challenge for the U.S. military and stated that it was an important reason "transformation" of the U.S. military needed to be accelerated. NDP (1997, pp. 11–13) noted that, since the United States depended on power projection to defend its global interests, it was vulnerable to an opponent's asymmetric efforts to deny it access to vital regions of the world. Such efforts might include the use of ballistic and cruise missiles (possibly fitted with chemical, biological, or nuclear warheads) to neutralize ports and airfields, forward bases, and prepositioned assets; the use of sea mines and antiship cruise missiles (ASCMs) to deny our use of key

---

[5] The downsizing of the U.S. military is another important factor in its ability to maintain a robust forward presence.

[6] The report of the 1997 QDR, in a discussion of asymmetric threats, states that if

an adversary ultimately faces a conventional war with the United States, it could also employ asymmetric means to delay or deny U.S. access to critical facilities; disrupt our command, control, communications, and intelligence networks; deter allies and potential coalition partners from supporting U.S. intervention; or inflict higher than expected U.S. casualties in an attempt to weaken our national resolve. (Cohen, 1997, p. 4) straits and littoral regions; attacks on fixed installations with standoff weapons; and efforts to divide us from our allies. WMD had particular salience because of their destructiveness, the perceived ease with which they could be acquired and used, and their purported ability to allow weak states to "counter and possibly thwart" the U.S. military's overwhelming conventional superiority and because traditional U.S. nuclear usage policies might no longer be sufficient to deter their use (NDP, 1997, pp. 15–16, 51). An important "transformational" capability was thus identified as the ability to project power into areas where the U.S. military lacked forward access (NDP, 1997, pp. 33–34, 35).

Four years after its tentative appearance in the report of the first QDR, and reflecting the concerns of the NDP, antiaccess was an important theme of the report of the 2001 QDR, which identified "projecting and sustaining U.S. forces in distant antiaccess or area-denial environments and defeating anti-access and area-denial threats" as one of six critical operational goals that should provide a focus for DoD's transformation efforts (Rumsfeld, 2001, p. 30). The 2001 QDR identified missiles (both ballistic and cruise) and chemical, biological, radiological, nuclear, and "enhanced high explosive" (CBRNE) weapons as the greatest antiaccess threats, particularly for their ability to deny or delay U.S. military access to overseas bases, airfields, and ports. Other antiaccess threats of concern included advanced air-defense systems that could threaten nonstealthy aircraft and advanced mines, ASCMs, and diesel submarines that could threaten the ability of U.S. naval and amphibious forces to operate in littoral waters (Rumsfeld, 2001, pp. 26, 31, 42, 43). Given these threats, and the fact that the U.S. defense strategy rests on the ability to project power globally, it was deemed vital that the U.S. military "retain the capability to send well-armed and logistically supported forces to critical points around the globe, even in the face of enemy opposition, or to locations where the support infrastructure is lacking or has collapsed" and that it monitor an opponent's ability to "detect and attack U.S. forces as they approach the conflict areas or hold at risk critical ports and air bases with missiles and CBRNE attacks" (Rumsfeld, 2001, p. 43). To enable the U.S. military to defeat the antiaccess threat, Rumsfeld (2001, pp. 43–44) deems theater missile defense necessary, as is addressing the growing threat posed by submarines, air defense systems, cruise missiles, and mines; accelerating development of the Army Objective Force; enhancing power projection and forcible entry capabilities; defeating long-range means of detection; enabling long-range attack capabilities; enhancing protection measures for strategic transport aircraft; and ensuring U.S. forces can sustain operations under chemical or biological attack.

According to public DoD comments, the need to counter the antiaccess threats identified in the QDR was subsequently included in the Defense Planning Guidance as a key operational goal of transformation (DoD, 2003).

More recently, similar language was included in the *Transformation Planning Guidance,* which called for a U.S. military able to "defeat the most potent of enemy anti-access and area denial capabilities through a combination of more-robust contamination avoidance measures, mobile basing and priority time critical counterforce targeting" (Rumsfeld, 2003, p. 10). Furthermore, transformation is explicitly linked to providing the capabilities the military requires to achieve the six critical operational goals, which include defeating antiaccess threats, identified in the 2001 QDR and the Defense Planning Guidance.

Using language similar to that of the 2001 QDR report (Rumsfeld, 2001, p. 30), the new defense strategy issued in March 2005 listed "projecting and sustaining forces in distant anti-access environments" as one of eight "key operational capabilities" (DoD, 2005, pp. 12–13). The report of the QDR based on this strategy that was issued a year later gave less explicit prominence to the antiaccess issue but did state that "the United States will continue to adapt its global posture to . . . mitigate anti-access threats" and that the U.S. military needs the following capabilities: "persistent surveillance, including systems that can penetrate and loiter in denied or contested areas"; "the capability to deploy rapidly, assemble, command, project, reconstitute, and reemploy joint combat power from all domains to facilitate assured access"; and "secure broadband communications into denied or contested areas to support penetrating surveillance and strike systems" (DoD, 2006, pp. 30–31).

The potential antiaccess threat is also an important theme in military service documents discussing transformation and future operational concepts. Both the Army's Stryker Brigade Combat Team and its Future Force have been motivated and justified in part by the need to be able to deploy into a theater of operations where traditional fixed deployment infrastructure may not exist or is threatened by enemy antiaccess capabilities. The U.S. Air Force, for its part, sees its Global Strike concept of operations (CONOPS) as a means to defeat the postulated antiaccess capabilities of potential adversaries. The Global Strike CONOPS is said to be designed to "enable joint forces to meet access and time challenges" and may include "neutralizing the adversary's anti-access systems, paving the way for follow-on persistent forces . . . needed to continue after the initial anti-access campaign" (Headquarters U.S. Air Force, 2004). Finally, the Navy's "Sea Shield" concept of operations is intended to defeat enemy antiaccess threats by providing mobile theater air and missile defense that will protect critical infrastructure ashore and littoral sea-control capabilities that can neutralize an opponent's advanced mine, diesel submarine, and swarming small combatant threats (U.S. Navy, 2003, pp. 3, 8, 17–22; Bucchi and Mullen, 2002, pp. 56–59).

It is thus clear that, since its tentative appearance in the 1997 QDR report, the antiaccess challenge has now become firmly embedded in future U.S. military modernization plans and high-level strategic documents.

Previous Analyses of the Antiaccess Threat

In 1996, the DSB noted its disappointment in the quality and quantity of work on the problem of the antiaccess threat.[7] Since that time, a growing body of studies on the antiaccess threat has emerged, but the overall quantity remains relatively small. This is striking, considering

---

[7]   DSB (1996, pp. 13, 53) used the term *force survivability*, but what the board was discussing is clearly identifiable as what is now described as the antiaccess threat.

the rich body of analytic work available examining the converse issue of "access."[8]

One notable feature of recent antiaccess studies is the large degree to which they reflect the antiaccess challenges laid out in both the 1996 DSB report and the 1997 NDP report. The primary problem remains the U.S. military's dependence on fixed airfields and ports for deployment and on theater airfields for the effective operation of tactical strike aircraft.[9] There is broad consensus on the primary antiaccess threats, with those most mentioned being long-range ballistic and cruise missiles, ASCMs, WMD (especially chemical and biological weapons), advanced sea mines, diesel submarines, and SOF. Ballistic missiles armed with WMD warheads are given particular prominence in the literature both because of their ability to bring deployment and combat operations to a halt at fixed bases and because of their potential use as a coercive tool to drive a wedge between the United States and countries that provide the U.S. military with access.

The closest thing to a comprehensive study of the antiaccess challenge is probably a 2003 report from the Center for Strategic and Budgetary Assessments (Krepinevich, Watts, and Work, 2003). This study analyzes at a general level the threat that antiaccess strategies and "area denial" operations—operations that "aim to prevent [U.S. forces'] freedom of action in the more-narrow confines of the area under an enemy's direct control" (Krepinevich, Watts, and Work, 2003, p. 5)—present to the operational approaches of each U.S. military service.

---

[8] The "access" literature focuses on the physical infrastructure, host-nation support, and logistics requirements of force deployment. Naturally, there is some overlap between the access and antiaccess literature. O'Malley (2001, pp. 23–29, 35–38), for instance, uses ballistic missile ranges as one of its criteria for determining the suitability of an airfield; Shlapak et al. (2002, pp. 40, 51–55) briefly discusses the role of fear and coercion in the politics of access and includes potential threat capabilities as a factor in choosing suitable airfields.

[9] Others have noted that aircraft carrier strike groups are dependent on bases ashore for their continuing combat effectiveness and that a clever opponent will seek to sever this vital link. A carrier strike group, for instance, requires regular deliveries of jet engines and repair parts to and from forward bases if it is to conduct prolonged operations. Furthermore, naval operations also depend on secure bases ashore for land-based maritime patrol operations (an important antisubmarine warfare [ASW] and intelligence-collection function), cruise missile replenishment, and repair facilities. (See Nagy, 1999, pp. 58–61.)

There have also been a number of valuable analyses of the effects of potential antiaccess methods on facets of the deployment chain. For example, Stanton (2001, pp. 54–57) discusses the potential vulnerability of U.S. naval combatants to unconventional attacks while in constrained waters, such as straits, canals, or ports. Similarly, Packard (2000) discusses the potential vulnerability of the U.S. Marine Corps's Afloat Prepositioning Force to attack by enemy SOF.

Despite the prominence that the antiaccess literature gives the vulnerability of fixed targets, particularly to missile attacks, this area has been subject to little comprehensive exploration. Most studies focus on the effects of a chemical or nuclear attack on such installations and ignore the effects of a more-probable conventional strike. A good example of this is the detailed examination of the threat to ports and air bases from chemical- and nuclear-armed missiles in Weaver and Glaes (1997), which argues that WMD are the tools of choice for regional powers to use against the critical fixed facilities required for U.S. power-projection operations. While one cannot discount the possibility of a WMD attack against U.S. installations, it is also important to thoroughly explore non-WMD threats to U.S. deployment operations and fixed installations.[10]

Fortunately, two excellent recent studies examine important facets of the problem of air base vulnerability. Stillion and Orletsky (1999) focuses narrowly on the threat to unsheltered aircraft and personnel from ballistic and cruise missiles armed with conventional anti-materiel submunition warheads and the operational problems of being forced to operate from bases outside the range of an enemy's missile force. Bowie (2002) takes a broader perspective, arguing that, over the long term, the combined uncertainties arising from both political factors and emerging military threats will tend to constrain the combat power of land-based fighter aircraft significantly. Bowie identifies the primary military threat as long-range cruise and ballistic missiles (what he labels "deep-strike systems"), SOF, and WMD. He also emphasizes the vulnerability of unsheltered aircraft and notes that it would

---

[10] Some argue that states can be deterred from using such weapons in a preemptive antiaccess role. For example, see Bowie (2002, pp. 50–51).

be difficult to close a runway for an extended period with either ballistic or cruise missiles, but fuel supplies and prepositioned ammunition ships would be lucrative and hard-to-protect targets.[11] Bowie also notes that, while hardening is expensive, closing hardened airfields for a substantial period requires using a large number of precision weapons (see Bowie, 2002, pp. 45, 54–55). Both studies suggest that long-range bombers are part of the solution to the antiaccess problem. A third relevant study, Shlapak and Vick (1995), does not explicitly address the antiaccess issue, but it does explore the threat to airfields and airfield operations from SOF units in detail.[12]

Concern about air base vulnerability, however, is not a recent phenomenon. In the mid-1980s, the threat from Soviet tactical aircraft led to concern within the U.S. Air Force about operating from forward locations that were under attack. The result was the 1985 Salty Demo exercise, which highlighted the chaos that sustained attacks (over 30 strikes per day) could create and led to policy recommendations on how to harden and prepare an airfield for flight operations while being subject to an enemy's attack (Correll, 1988; Bowie, 2002, p. 47).[13]

While airfields have has some analytic treatment, the issue of vulnerability of ports to conventional attacks seems to have been largely overlooked. In one article, Siegel (2002, pp. 34–36) notes that even a single lucky shot on a crowded port, if it hits an ammunition stockpile or ship, has the potential to cause a great deal of damage to a port.[14] In

---

[11] Bowie (2002, p. 28) notes that a week's supply of current-generation weapons for three "air expeditionary forces" weighs about 20,000 short tons, the equivalent of the 82nd Airborne Division plus three days' worth of supplies.

[12] An interesting companion piece to this work is Vick (1995), which looks at the historical threat to air bases from ground attacks.

[13] Another good discussion of air base attack can be found in Halliday (1987), which examines how three days of attacks by one or two Soviet regiments of aircraft (36 or 72 aircraft) would affect the sortie rates and aircraft inventory of a U.S. Air Force fighter wing.

[14] Siegel takes only a brief look at a potential problem, however, and it is unclear whether his conclusion about the amount of damage from exploding ammunition would hold up under a more-detailed analysis of the damage mechanism being posited.

general, however, there appear to be few if any studies of the vulnerability of ports to conventional attack.[15]

In addition to military threats to access, there are potentially important political ones.[16] Historically, the primary reason the United States has lost access to theater bases has been a divergence between host-nation and U.S. national interests (Coté, 2001, pp. 2, 12–13). The United States lost access to important bases in the Philippines and Panama because of domestic political opposition to its presence.[17] More recently, the Turkish Parliament rejected a U.S. request to launch a northern front against Iraq during Operation Iraqi Freedom. While these particular events were primarily due to purely internal political forces, an adversary of the United States could potentially attempt to cause a similar effect by using diplomatic suasion to convince a key nation in its region to deny U.S. forces the right to operate from or through that nation's territory in the event of a conflict between the adversary and the United States.[18] Indeed, Larson et al. (2003, pp. xv–xvi, 97–98) identified an opponent's ability to exploit such divergences of interest as one of the key antiaccess threats the United States faces. Another potential U.S. political vulnerability is the trend away from formal alliances that assure access and provide security guarantees, such as the North Atlantic Treaty Organization (NATO), toward more *ad hoc* relationships that are created as required and involve few military commitments on the part of the United States (Coté, 2001, pp. 8–9). The need to create such relationships "on the fly" could increase an opponent's ability to drive a wedge between the United States and its potential partners and thus could lead either to the denial of required

---

[15] The technical aspects of port vulnerability and repair can be found in Smith, Cooksey, et al. (1988).

[16] Blaker (1990) examines the importance of overseas bases and the international political issues involved in securing basing rights.

[17] On the Philippines, see Cruz de Castro (2003, pp. 971–988).

[18] The United States does, of course, have powerful tools, such as power, prestige, and money, with which to counter such efforts (see Bowie, 2002, pp. 32–33). Some Air Force advocates have long argued that "access" is not an issue because the United States has never been prevented from conducting significant military operations to which it was seriously committed (see "The Access Issue," 1998).

access or to a militarily significant delay in its granting. The political antiaccess threat is thus as serious as the military one.

Most of these studies, however, have focused on generic threats to U.S. access. There has no been no in-depth assessment of what types of antiaccess tactics and strategies specific countries might employ in a conflict with the United States. The antiaccess analyses that examine specific scenarios generally assume that the adversary in question would use the adversary's capabilities to deny U.S. forces access in the same way as the (American) analysts would. At most, they have relied on a nonsystematic examination of a country's doctrinal writings for ideas about what types of antiaccess methods that country might employ. In particular, there has been no in-depth analysis of what types of antiaccess methods the military strategists of one of the most prominent candidates for employing such an approach might be contemplating—China.

Definition of Antiaccess

Despite the high-level interest in antiaccess and the term's increasing use in U.S. defense policy documents, no official definition of either "antiaccess" or an "antiaccess strategy" exists.[19] For purposes of this study, we considered an *antiaccess measure* to be any action by an opponent that has the effect of slowing the deployment of friendly forces into a theater, preventing them from operating from certain locations within that theater, or causing them to operate from distances farther from the locus of conflict than they would normally prefer.[20]

Examples of antiaccess measures include attacks on airfields, which could force aircraft to operate from more-remote airfields or could prevent additional forces from being flown into the theater; attacks on seaports, which could prevent additional forces from being brought into the theater through these ports; and attacks on aircraft

---

[19] The terms *access* and *antiaccess* cannot be found in the DoD dictionary (DoD, 2001, as amended).

[20] See Larson et al. (2003) for a differently worded but essentially similar definition.

carriers, which could prevent naval aviation from operating within the theater or force the carriers to withdraw to more-distant locations from which their aircraft would be less effective. Examples of what were not considered antiaccess measures include efforts at camouflage and concealment, short-range air defenses, or defensive combat air patrols because, while these measures might render U.S. attacks within a given area more risky or less effective and could even deter U.S. forces from striking targets in that area, they would not impede the deployment of friendly forces into the overall theater of conflict or force them to operate from more-distant locations.

Approach

This monograph describes the types of antiaccess measures China might employ in a future conflict with the United States, their potential consequences, and actions the United States can take and capabilities it should acquire to reduce these consequences. We identified the types of antiaccess measures China might employ in a future conflict with the United States by examining Chinese military doctrinal writings for descriptions of actions that, in the event of a conflict between the United States and China, could impede U.S. access to the western Pacific. These writings were found in openly published and internally distributed Chinese-language books on military strategy, articles in Chinese military journals, reports from Chinese military newspapers, and recent Western studies of Chinese security policy.[21]

Chinese writings on military and security issues have proliferated in recent years, presenting analysts of the Chinese military, once handicapped by a lack of primary source materials, with an almost overwhelming amount of new information and a wide range of new research opportunities (see Medeiros, 2003, pp. 119–168). In addition

---

[21] The last include Ross (2002, pp. 48–85), Christensen (2001, pp. 5–40), Pillsbury (2000), and Pillsbury (1998). Because of the unlikelihood that members of China's defense establishment would be willing to speak to RAND researchers on such a sensitive topic, we did not attempt to interview Chinese military strategists for this project but instead incorporated information from interviews conducted in other contexts when relevant.

to the growing availability of Chinese-language books and journal articles on military affairs, a rapidly expanding universe of information about the People's Liberation Army (PLA) and Chinese security policy is also available on the Internet.[22] These new sources have yielded new insights in many areas of research on the PLA, including strategy and doctrine, training, and defense economics.[23]

While these materials promise to revolutionize research on the PLA and Chinese military affairs, they also present analysts with several formidable challenges, one of the most significant of which is assessing the authoritativeness of sources.[24] We used two criteria for selecting the publications to read and evaluate for this report. First was whether a given source reflected authoritative PLA views or simply represented the personal opinions and views of the publication's author.[25] This is a particularly critical challenge because publications in China are no longer required to bear an official imprimatur or represent official views. On the contrary, there is an emerging group of civilian and military authors who aspire to be foreign policy and security pundits and who often express personal views in their writings, in quotes in official print media, and in television sound bites that may or may not have official sanction.

The second criterion was whether a publication appeared to target a professional audience or a wider readership. Many newsstand magazines are aimed at what seems to be a growing audience of amateur military enthusiasts in China, and the articles they carry are of highly variable reliability. At the other end of the spectrum are books clearly intended to be read by military officers and other professional defense specialists. Books printed by the publishing houses affiliated with the

---

[22] For a comprehensive assessment of the potential influence of Internet sources, as well as some of the difficulties the exploitation of such sources presents to analysts of the PLA, see Fravel (2003, pp. 49–118). For a more-general overview of the Chinese-language resources available on the Internet, see Fravel (2000, pp. 821–842).

[23] For more, see Medeiros (2005, pp. 132–137).

[24] For more on these challenges, see Medeiros (2003) and Finkelstein (2002, pp. 22–26).

[25] For more on the challenges and importance of making this distinction, see Finkelstein (2002, pp. 22–26).

PLA's National Defense University and Academy of Military Sciences (AMS) were considered to be among the sources most likely to reflect the mainstream views of high-level military personnel and security strategists.

Although the textual sources we analyzed for this study are authoritative examples of official Chinese military thinking, it is important to bear in mind that they are essentially theoretical. As other analysts have wisely cautioned, there may be a significant divergence between the views set forth in these theoretical publications and the actual practice of the PLA's "operational art" (Finkelstein, 2002, pp. 22–26). It should also be recognized that the set of Chinese military doctrinal writings reviewed for this study was undoubtedly incomplete. We were unable to acquire all the books and journals we wanted to review as part of this study, and it is highly likely that there are additional relevant Chinese military doctrinal publications that we are unaware of.

In addition, the Chinese military writings analyzed for this study were general doctrinal texts, not specific Chinese operational plans for conducting operations against the United States. In the absence of access to such operational plans, which the Chinese government would obviously do its utmost to protect, it is impossible to know precisely how the Chinese military would actually carry out the types of antiaccess measures these texts imply. In particular, it is possible that some of the tactics for defeating more technologically advanced militaries described in these writings were developed with Taiwan in mind, not the United States. Indeed, in some cases, China does not currently possess the capability to employ the tactics mentioned in the writings against the United States. As China's capabilities improve in the future, however, it is certainly reasonable to assume that they would be employed against the United States as well. Even if a particular tactic was conceived of or is discussed as specifically for use against Taiwan, we assumed that China would, when and if China acquired the requisite capability, use that tactic against the United States, unless there was a particular reason *not* to do so. If a vulnerability exists and if China has both the capability and an expressed intent to implement actions consistent with exploiting that vulnerability, it would be imprudent to assume that China would not do so.

A related point is that, in the same way that the extent to which these writings are intended to apply to the United States is often unclear, it is also often unclear whether these writings are specifically about Taiwan scenarios, since that is by far the most likely major conventional military contingency for China to become involved in at present, or are intended to be more generally applicable. Again, even if a particular tactic was conceived of or is discussed as specifically for use in a Taiwan scenario, we assumed that China would likely do so unless there is a particular reason that tactic would *not* be used in other scenarios.

It should be noted that the military doctrinal writings we examined do not reflect Chinese analyses of the performance of the U.S. military in Operation Enduring Freedom or Operation Iraqi Freedom. These operations are too recent to have affected official military doctrinal writings examined in this study—any formal changes to Chinese doctrine as a result of analyses of these operations will probably not appear until several years after these operations, as was the case after Operation Desert Storm in 1991.[26]

We determined the potential effects of the antiaccess measures from these Chinese military-doctrinal writings by assessing the actual capability of the Chinese military to implement these measures, taking into consideration the geography of the western Pacific and the U.S. basing structure in the region and analyzing how such implementation would affect U.S. military operations. We consulted RAND Corporation and external experts on military operations during this assessment and conducted a daylong seminar that presented a hypothetical U.S.-China conflict scenario to a group of RAND specialists on military operations and active-duty members of the U.S. military. Attendees described probable U.S. operational approaches to the conflict and assessed the likely effects of Chinese antiaccess measures on U.S. operations.

Finally, the actions the United States can take and the capabilities it should acquire to reduce the effects of Chinese antiaccess measures

---

[26] For a review of initial Chinese analyses of Operation Iraqi Freedom, see Albert et al. (2003).

were largely developed through consultation with RAND and external experts on the associated areas of military operations. This included the daylong seminar examining a hypothetical U.S.-China conflict scenario, which considered not just the likely effects of Chinese antiaccess measures but also actions the United States could take and capabilities it could acquire to counter them.

CHAPTER TWO

Contemporary Chinese Military Strategy

The bulk of Chinese writings on military strategy focus on such topics as amphibious operations; missile campaigns; joint operations; defensive information warfare; air defense; concealment, denial, and deception; psychological operations; and modernization of its command, control, communications, computers, intelligence, surveillance, and reconnaissance (C⁴ISR) systems. Antiaccess is not a distinct topic in these writings. The Chinese military publications we analyzed for this study do not appear to even use a term equivalent to *antiaccess* or refer to the considerable body of U.S. writings on the topic. Close analysis of Chinese military publications, however, including internal and openly published books, journal articles, and military newspaper reports, indicates that the strategies China is likely to employ in a conflict with the United States will contain prominent antiaccess elements. Indeed, antiaccess themes are pronounced when Chinese strategists discuss options available to the PLA for wresting the initiative from the United States or for preventing the timely deployment of additional U.S. forces in Asia.

This chapter provides an overview of Chinese strategists' view of the nature of warfare in the current security environment, the PLA's military limitations in the context of that security environment, and their overall assessment of U.S. military power. It then describes overall strategic principles Chinese military writers identify as important for the PLA to be able to confront a technologically superior adversary effectively in a military conflict and Chinese perceptions of vulnerabilities in the U.S. approach to warfare. The chapter that follows describes some of the specific strategies and tactics Chinese military sources discuss that have the potential to affect U.S. access to the Asia-Pacific region in the event of conflict with China.

Sources of Chinese Strategy

When contemplating the most effective way to contend with the U.S. military, Chinese strategic thinking is largely shaped by three separate aspects of China's current security environment: the likely nature of future military conflict, the limitations of China's current military capabilities, and the overwhelming military dominance of the United States.

"Local War Under High-Technology Conditions"

Like many things in China, the official view of the nature and demands of warfare has changed radically since the initiation of China's economic and political reform program in the late 1970s. Chinese views of warfare have evolved in response to their changing assessment of the international environment and the nature of the threats China must confront in that environment. This view of modern warfare, in turn, has shaped the military doctrine China has developed to protect and assert the nation's interests in the new environment.

Since 1976, the PLA's operational doctrine has evolved from advocating a largely defensive war based on using China's strategic depth and massive population to gradually wear down an opponent to an offensive strategy based on the rapid projection of force in response to external threats and seizing the initiative at the outset of conflict. China's national military strategy has shifted from continental defense to defending areas on China's periphery and to maritime force projection. One important consequence of this change in military strategy is that it has forced the PLA, traditionally a low-tech military geared toward guerrilla warfare and massed infantry tactics, to come to grips with its inadequacies in conducting warfare that places a premium on mobility, rapid operations, and modern precision weaponry.

From 1978 to 1985, the PLA described the type of war it expected to fight as "people's war under modern conditions." Its primary focus was on how to defend China from a limited invasion by the Soviet Union aimed at key political and industrial centers in north China. While the PLA continued to rely on massing large armies to repel invaders, it could no longer rely on luring an enemy deep within its territory to weaken its adversary. Although China was still a largely agrarian society, important economic and political centers had emerged in the second half of the 20th century that had to be defended. By the late 1970s, Chinese military strategists were concerned that, in the event of war with the Soviet Union, Soviet military forces would not seek to invade all of China but, rather, simply choose to occupy China's important industrial centers in its northeastern provinces, near its borders with the Soviet Union.

In response to these perceived changes in the security threat it confronted, the PLA planned to defend China at its borders with a strategy of "active defense." As then-president of AMS Xiao Ke put it,

> to follow the method of "luring the enemy in deep" used by the Red Army during the Jiangxi period and apply it mechanically would be absurd. At that time we occupied no cities and had no modern industry; we took everything needed from the enemy.[1]

Instead, the PLA would conduct a series of blocking actions meant to channel the Soviet Army into battlefields of the PLA's choosing. While China's conventional military forces kept the Soviets occupied, guerrilla forces would maneuver behind the main Soviet force to attack logistics targets to wear down the Soviet assault. Once Soviet forces had weakened, the PLA would conduct counterattacks against the Soviets.

As the geopolitical situation changed in the 1980s, so did Chinese doctrine. In 1985, Chinese strategists concluded that, because of the Soviet Union's preoccupation with countering the United States, war with the Soviet Union was unlikely. While war with the Soviet Union was not excluded, it was believed that any military confrontation with

---

[1]   From Xinhua, September 9, 1979, cited in Godwin (2001, p. 91).

the Soviet Union would be limited in geographical scope and political objective. Military planners also began to envision other contingencies along China's borders that might require military action. PLA theorists predicted that these new contingencies would be "local, limited wars" with an objective to "assert one's own standpoint and will through limited military action" rather than complete annihilation of an adversary's capabilities (Jiao and Xiao, 1987; quoted in Godwin, 1992, p. 194). Chinese military planners expected these wars to be short and believed that they would be determined not only by military action but also by political and diplomatic factors.

Preparing for local, limited wars that could break out in a variety of locales presented the PLA with many challenges. Instead of focusing on an invasion from the north, China now also had to consider using its military around the entirety of its periphery, including the ocean. Operationally, the PLA emphasized offensive operations that could bring about a rapid decision to a conflict, rather than engaging in a protracted war. It established better-trained and -equipped rapid-reaction forces and "fist units" to respond quickly to contingencies and began to emphasize joint operations, which for the first time eroded the dominance of the ground forces in Chinese strategy (Godwin, 1999, p. 54).

The overwhelming success of the United States–led invasion of Iraq during the Gulf War in 1991, however, forced Chinese analysts to reconsider their ability to fight an opponent armed with advanced weaponry. The Gulf War did conform to the Chinese view of modern wars as being quick and intense, but the effectiveness with which the U.S. military used airpower and joint operations to paralyze an Iraqi army that was in some cases armed with Chinese weapons caused concern within the PLA that it was woefully unprepared, in terms of both technology and operational doctrine, to fight and win a similar type of war.[2] As one analyst of Chinese doctrine (Godwin, 1999, p. 55) writes,

---

[2]   According to International Institute for Strategic Studies (1990), Chinese-made weaponry in Iraq's inventory included 1,500 Type 59 and Type 69 tanks, 1,000 YW-531 armored

[w]hat PLA analysts saw was not a war of the future, but a war as it could be fought today by a post-industrial power. Little the PLA had achieved by reorganization, modifying its force structure, building a better educated officer corps, reconceptualizing the manner it planned to conduct future wars, and more realistic training could offset the impact of technology on operations by well-trained, properly organized joint forces exploiting the technological sophistication of their armaments and supporting systems.

PLA analysis of the Gulf War paid considerable attention to the role of the U.S. military's reconnaissance and surveillance assets. The role of airpower received attention for its ability to destroy air defense and command-and-control nodes, while the U.S. use of stealth aircraft and cruise missiles highlighted the difficulties the PLA would have in defending itself against an attack from an advanced air force (Sun Lihui, 2002).

In 1993, President Jiang Zemin directed the PLA to focus on preparing to fight 高技术条件下局部战争 ["local wars under high-technology conditions"]. As the term suggests, there are two discrete components to this concept, each the product of distinct trends in the international security environment. Local wars under modern high-technology conditions, also called 高技术局部战争 ["high-technology local wars"], are (1) limited in geographical scope, duration, and political objectives and (2) dominated by high-technology weaponry. They feature highly accurate and lethal firepower; the joint use of air, land, and sea forces; the intense use of information technology; and high mobility, lethality, and resource consumption. High-technology local wars are also characterized by near-total battlefield awareness, nonlinear battlefields, and multidimensional combat (Finkelstein, 1999, pp. 127–128).

Local wars differ fundamentally from *total war*, the type of warfare that the PLA traditionally prepared to fight. In total war, the PLA's objective would have been the total destruction of all threatening enemy forces, who, in turn, would have been bent on the complete

---

personnel carriers, an unspecified number of Type 59-1 howitzers, and 60 J-6 and 40 J-7 fighters.

destruction of the Chinese communist state. In contrast, PLA theorists assess that local wars are characterized by the pursuit of limited political goals through relatively limited use of force.[3] Military force is more of an adjunct to diplomatic strategies aimed at achieving or defending discrete political objectives. According to Peng and Yao (2001, p. 451), in local wars, "what is emphasized most is the combined use of many types of military, political, economic, and diplomatic measures" [authors' translation]. Military action is intended to create conditions for the achievement of the desired political outcome.

Chinese strategists formally began to use the term *high-technology* to describe contemporary warfare following the first Gulf War. *High-technology* is the general label Chinese writers use to describe advances in the range, precision, and destructiveness of modern weapon systems, as well as in the effectiveness and integration of reconnaissance and communication capabilities. While Chinese strategists had emphasized the role of technology in warfare since the late 1970s, the U.S. performance in the first Gulf War made a deep impression on them. As one Chinese official has noted (Ding, 1995),

> the Gulf War demonstrated that the application of high-tech in the military has given weapons an unprecedented degree of precision and power, heightening the suddenness, three dimensionality, mobility, rapidity, and depth of modern warfare.

The U.S. military's devastation of Iraq's army, which was mostly equipped with Soviet and Chinese weaponry, offered Chinese observers sobering proof of high-technology weaponry's ability to deliver highly accurate, lethal firepower and thereby bring about a rapid decision on the battlefield.

Although there have been important advances across a wide range of weaponry-related technology, Chinese military analysts consider information technology to be what truly differentiates high-technology warfare from earlier forms of warfare. As one Chinese general explains, "information equipment of all kinds is linked into wide-ranging networks, forming huge information systems with C⁴ISR systems at their

---

[3]   See, for example, Peng and Yao (2001, pp. 435–437, 450–452, 487–488).

core, becoming the nerve center of a modern armed force" (Dai, 2002). Improvements in sensor, communication, and guidance technologies allow a high-technology military to gather and utilize information about the battlefield more rapidly and effectively than ever before. As impressive as such individual U.S. platforms as the B-2 stealth bomber are, Chinese analysts believe that U.S. military superiority actually rests on its effective use of information technology (its C^{4}ISR network).

Ultimately, the distinct trends of "local war" and "high-technology conditions" have similar and mutually reinforcing effects on the nature of war. Foremost among these is to make wars short, perhaps consisting of a single campaign that will be highly destructive and decided quickly. This implies that victory in the opening battle may decide a war (Li, 1999, pp. 149–150).

Operationally, high-technology local wars create an imperative that a military be able to seize and hold the initiative from the outset of hostilities. High-technology local wars offer little opportunity for one side to present an effective defense if it finds itself disadvantaged following an initial onslaught. In the words of one Chinese analyst, "in a limited high-tech war, where the pace of action is fast and the duration short, a campaign often takes on a make-or-break character. Clearly the quick and decisive battle assumes much more importance in such a war" (Lu, 1996). Once lost, it is all but impossible for a country to regain the initiative.[4]

China's Military Weaknesses

Although China has made considerable progress in military modernization, the demands of high-technology local warfare present a wide range of serious challenges to the PLA. Through most of its existence, the PLA had prepared for warfare that would be conducted on the mainland itself, where its overwhelming numbers, coupled with Chi-

---

[4] Since December 2004, the terms *local war under high-technology conditions* and *high-technology local war* have been replaced in Chinese doctrinal writings by the term 信息化战争 [*informationalized war*]. This new concept emerged after the bulk of the research for this project had been completed, however, and the doctrinal implications between *high-technology local war* and *informationalized war* were not fully clear at the time this study was completed.

na's geographic vastness, would eventually wear down an invading force. High-technology local war requires something dramatically different. The PLA needs to be able to project power rapidly to its periphery or beyond, to confront an adversary that likely has technologically superior weaponry and probably has no intention of trying to take and hold territory on the mainland.

Many Chinese writers and strategists are under no illusions regarding the PLA's shortcomings, including the quality of training, the educational level of PLA personnel, and even doctrinal issues.

The challenges China will face in a high-technology local war are compounded by the PLA's technological and doctrinal shortcomings. Internal assessments of the state of the Chinese military modernization assert that the PLA has yet to fully develop "mechanized" warfare capabilities similar to those the United States and the Soviet Union deployed up to the late 1970s, to say nothing of the ability to prosecute an "informationized (high-technology)" war effectively (Xu, 2002; Li, 2000; Yang, 1998). Given these realities, many Chinese strategists concede that high-technology local war presents the PLA with "grim challenges" (Li, 1998).

Chinese analysts also bluntly acknowledge that China's military technology is inferior to that of its most likely potential adversaries and that this situation will not change for the foreseeable future.[5] As a passage in Peng and Yao (2001, p. 466) explains,

> the most salient objective reality that the PLA will face in future campaign operations is the fact that it will be using inferior weapons to deal with an enemy that has superior arms. [authors' translation]

The passage goes on to note that the PLA's "guiding concepts" for military planning need to be developed with "a clear recognition of this reality" (Peng and Yao, 2001, p. 467 [authors' translation]). Chinese analysts also acknowledge that one consequence of this deficiency is that China will likely absorb a great deal of damage and must be will-

---

[5]   See, for example, Peng and Yao (2001, pp. 466–467).

ing to "pay a heavy price" in any conflict with a technologically superior adversary, such as the United States.[6]

Chinese strategists point in particular to weaknesses in the PLA's long-range precision-strike capabilities. According to Wang and Zhang (2000, p. 25),

> in view of actual conditions, the PLA in a short time or in a considerably long time will not possess the 纵深立体打击能力 [deep and multidirectional strike capabilities] of the world's top military powers. [authors' translation]

The PLA has also suffered from doctrinal weaknesses, according to a number of Chinese writers. Aside from the challenging materiel demands of high-technology local war, Chinese strategists must also develop new strategies, tactics, and principles to guide how the PLA will train for and operate in future military conflicts. The doctrinal transition from People's War to a military strategy more suitable to high-technology local war has not been smooth or clear. As one article in *Chinese Military Science* noted, the PLA has "yet to solve" the challenge of "freeing itself from the influence of old conventions, familiar rules, and outdated concepts" (Huang and Zuo, 1996, pp. 49–56). As described earlier, high-technology local war entails a range of operational requirements very different from the sort called for by the PLA's older, People's War doctrine.[7]

U.S. Military Technological Superiority

One of the most persistent themes in Chinese military writings is that many, if not most, of the PLA's potential adversaries are substantially more advanced than the PLA in terms of military technology.[8] Nowhere is the gap in military technology more severe than between the PLA

---

[6] See, for example, Jiang (1997, pp. 111–112).

[7] In 1999, the PLA issued a new set of operational regulations. At the time that the analysis for this study was conducted, it was not yet clear whether PLA analysts assessed these new regulations to have fully resolved its doctrinal shortcomings (see Finkelstein, 2002).

[8] The PLA has often faced or prepared to face technologically superior adversaries, and this has historically been an important theme in Chinese writings on strategy and doctrine. For

and the U.S. military. Chinese military analysts recognize that contending with U.S. military power in a local war will pose extreme challenges for the PLA, particularly within the context of high-technology local war (Godwin, 2001).[9]

Chinese strategists also acknowledge that the United States sets the standard for military power in today's world. The United States has been at the center of the information revolution, which in turn forms the technological basis of high-technology local war. Perhaps more importantly, the U.S. military has demonstrated the ability to use that technology to enhance its overall combat effectiveness to a far greater extent than any other military. Chinese Lieutenant General Li Jijun illustrates this recognition of U.S. military power in describing the U.S. performance in the first Gulf War, noting that it demonstrated "great strategy, great command, great logistics, and a great alliance forming a great system." General Li concludes that the U.S. performance represented a "big step forward in both military theory and practice" (Shi, 1995, pp. 70–76).

At the same time, Chinese military leaders understand that a very real possibility exists that China will have to confront that same U.S. military if it is going to preserve or affirm what Beijing believes are its sovereign rights over Taiwan. Knowledge of their weakness relative to U.S. military power is insufficient to compel Chinese leaders to renounce interests that might bring them into conflict with the United States. It is important to understand, therefore, what Chinese strategists consider to be the strategic principles for defeating a technologically superior adversary.

---

more on developments in Chinese doctrine from the Korean War to the period after the Gulf War, see Godwin (2001, pp. 87–118).

[9]   Godwin cites an article by a PLA analyst who asserts that there are no historical cases in which a country with a technologically inferior military has defeated a technologically superior adversary in a high-technology local war.

Strategic Principles for Defeating a Technologically Superior Adversary

It is apparent that many Chinese strategists recognize the scope of the challenges the PLA must confront, as described above. These strategists understand that the nature of warfare has changed in a way that renders China's traditional strengths, such as its strategic depth, all but irrelevant. They also appear to understand that the PLA has to develop rapid-reaction and force-projection capabilities that its technology base and, to a lesser extent, operational doctrine cannot currently support. Finally, they recognize that one of their most likely adversaries, the United States, is superior to the PLA in almost all aspects of high-technology local war and that the dangers the PLA would have to confront in an open conflict with the U.S. military would be extreme.

Chinese military writings suggest that the PLA's strategic approach to these challenges has coalesced around a number of discrete themes. Articles in Chinese military journals and publications describe a range of strategies and tactics designed to maximize China's chances of prevailing in a high-technology local war against the United States.

Underlying the Chinese approach toward a potential conflict with the United States is the conviction that even an adversary with superior weapons, technology, and equipment will be unable to maintain absolute superiority in all respects. Military conflict does not occur in a vacuum. Rather, it takes place within a specific geographic and political context that will inevitably provide the PLA with opportunities to offset the United States' advantages in technology. As Jiang (1997, pp. 113–114) explains,

> if China confronts an enemy with high technology and superior equipment in a local war, it is impossible that the enemy would also have comprehensive superiority in politics, diplomacy, geography, and support. [authors' translation]

In considering all the factors that have an influence on the outcome of a conflict, "apart from its technological superiority, it would be difficult for the enemy to gain superiority in all of these other respects." As a result, "there are opportunities to defeat even adversaries with the most advanced weaponry and equipment" (Jiang, 1997, p. 112 [authors' translation]).[10]

The central challenge for Chinese military planners, therefore, is to devise strategies that will maximize China's relative strengths and create opportunities to exploit U.S. weaknesses. This is reiterated in numerous sources, including an internal volume on the study of campaigns, which states that "only by using its areas of strength to strike at the enemy's weakness can the PLA achieve campaign victory in future wars against aggression" (Wang and Zhang, 2000, p. 25 [authors' translation]).

Avoiding Direct Confrontation

Chinese strategists appear to understand that success against the U.S. military depends on China's ability to avoid a direct confrontation with U.S. forces in a traditional, force-on-force battle. In an interview with the newspaper *China Youth Daily*, a PLA senior colonel compared any attempt by China to contend directly with the United States in a high-technology conflict to "throwing an egg against a rock" (Sha, 1999). This sentiment is echoed broadly (although less colorfully) in a number of articles appearing in more-authoritative journals. The conclusion these articles stress is that the PLA must develop operational doctrine and combat capabilities that will allow it to exploit U.S. vulnerabilities decisively.[11]

Seizing the Initiative Early

No principle is as routinely and uniformly emphasized in Chinese writings on the demands of high-technology local war as the need for the PLA to seize the initiative from the outset of a conflict. Although official Chinese doctrine holds that, at the strategic level, China will never

---

[10] For one example among the many sources that address this topic, see Jiang (1997). On pp. 35–41, Jiang discusses the PLA's history of fighting against enemies with superior equipment and technology in the Chinese civil war, the war against Japan, and the Korean War. In addition, Jiang notes that it was Mao Zedong who, at a meeting in September 1953, first officially raised the formulation of 以劣势装备战胜优势装备之敌 ["using inferior equipment to defeat an enemy with superior equipment"].

[11] See, for example, Shen (1998, pp. 218–219).

initiate a conflict, Chinese military observers view seizing the initiative at the operational level to be an imperative if they hope to have any chance of success, particularly against an adversary as potent as the United States. As one *Liberation Army Daily* article argues, "in a high-tech local war, a belligerent which adopts a passive defensive strategy and launches no offensive against the enemy is bound to fold its hands and await destruction" (Huang, 1999, p. 6).

The risks of passively waiting for the enemy to complete deployment and buildup of forces are potentially devastating. Once the U.S. marshals its forces, the PLA would find itself in an untenable position. In the words of one Chinese analyst (Lu, 1996),

> if [the PLA] just sits there and waits for the enemy to complete assembling its full array of troops, China's fighting potential will certainly be more severely jeopardized because the enemy will then be in a position to put its overall combat superiority to good use, making it more difficult for China to win the war.

Moreover, "for the weaker party, waiting for the enemy to deliver the first blow will have disastrous consequences and may even put it in a passive situation from which it will never be able to get out" (Lu, 1996).

Surprise

Chinese strategists recognize that attaining some degree of surprise may be necessary to effectively seize the initiative in a conflict with an adversary as powerful as the United States. Indeed, numerous Chinese strategists emphasize 出奇制胜 [achieving victory through surprise] by striking at an unexpected time and in an unanticipated place.[12] In one recent internal volume (Wang and Zhang, 2000, pp. 108–110), Chinese military writers highlight the importance of surprise, defining it and describing its potential results as follows:

> Taking the enemy by surprise would catch it unprepared and cause confusion within and huge psychological pressure on the

---

[12] See, for instance, Peng and Yao (2001, p. 307).

enemy and would help one win relatively large victories at relatively small costs. [authors' translation]

Wang and Zhang (2000, pp. 108–110) further states that, once surprise is achieved, the PLA must exploit it decisively as quickly as possible:

> Under modern conditions, it is difficult to sustain surprise, which can only exist at the beginning. Therefore, once surprise is achieved, one must move quickly to exploit and expand the initial battle success, so as not to let the enemy regain its footing from the confusion. [authors' translation]

How China will be able to conduct such operations in the face of the clear superiority the U.S. military holds over Chinese forces remains a problem. Chinese analysts express their concerns that surprise is becoming more difficult to achieve, although they assess that it is still possible. According to Wang and Zhang (2000, pp. 108–110),

> disguising one's own intent well is an important element of taking the enemy by surprise. The objective of disguising one's intent can be achieved through camouflage, deception, feint, and under bad weather. Although it has become more difficult to disguise one's intent under modern conditions, modern campaign practice has proved that it is still possible to take the enemy by surprise through excellent stratagem, smart camouflage, deception, feint, and under bad weather conditions. With developments in disguising technology and equipment, it is particularly important to deceive and mislead the enemy by high-technology means so as to truly hide one's intent and achieve victory by taking the enemy by surprise. [authors' translation]

In terms of timing, it is critical to strike before the superior adversary has a chance to initiate its own attack or when it is still deploying its forces and building up its strength. According to one Chinese writer, "the enemy is most vulnerable during the early phase of the war when it is still deploying troops and making operational preparations" (Lu, 1996). Similarly, the authors of a Chinese book on U.S. military strategy (Pan and Sun, 1994, p. 238) view the deployment phase as a critical period of weakness for the United States:

> In the opening stage, it is impossible to rapidly transfer enormous forces to the battlefield. Thus [the United States] is unable to establish superiority of forces and firepower, and it is easy for the U.S. military to be forced into a passive position from the start; this could very possibly have an impact on the process and outcome of the conflict. [authors' translation]

To this end, one possibility mentioned in an internal volume is using a military exercise as 掩护 [cover] for the preparations that would precede an attack (Wang and Zhang, 2000, p. 330). This is the point at which the logic of preemptive attack begins to assert itself in Chinese writings.

Preemption

A number of Chinese authors describe preemptive attack as a necessary and logical strategy for a less-advanced country to utilize against a more-powerful adversary. If future wars will be decided largely by the outcome of the initial engagement or campaign, attempting to take the initiative after hostilities have commenced seems a risky strategy, particularly for the weaker side. A quick strike prior to or quickly following the formal declaration of hostilities will disrupt U.S. deployment of forces to the region, place the United States in a passive position, and deliver a psychological shock to the United States and its allies. As Lu (1996) argues,

> this makes it imperative that China launch a preemptive strike by taking advantage of the window of opportunity present before the enemy acquires a high-tech edge or develops a full-fledged combat capability in the war zone. Through a preemptive strike, China can put good timing and geographical location and the support of the people to good use by making a series of offensive moves to destroy the enemy's ability to deploy high-tech weapons and troops and limit its ability to acquire a high-tech edge in the war zone, thus weakening its capacity to mount a powerful offen-

sive. This is the only way to steer the course of the war in a direction favorable to China.

Iraq's fate in the first Gulf War provided ample evidence to Chinese strategists of the perils of not seizing the initiative from the beginning of the conflict. Many Chinese assessments of the first Gulf War argue that Iraq would have had a better chance of defeating the United States if it had launched a preemptive attack instead of waiting for the United States to deliver the first blow. Chinese analysts assess that Iraq missed the opportunity to attack U.S. and coalition forces while they were deploying to the region (Jiang, 1997, pp. 151–152). According to Lu (1996),

> in the Gulf War, Iraq suffered from passive strategic guidance and overlooked the importance of seizing the initiative and launching a preemptive attack. In doing so, it missed a good opportunity to turn the war around and change its outcome.

For the PLA, the U.S. deployment phase represents a window of opportunity that can be exploited through preemptive attack. Accordingly, one Chinese analyst wrote the following (Lu, 1996):

> an effective strategy by which the weaker party can overcome its more-powerful enemy is to take advantage of serious gaps in the deployment of forces by the enemy with a high-tech edge by launching a preemptive strike during the early phase of the war or in the preparations leading to the offensive.

In the words of another Chinese analyst (Li, 1995, p. 190),

> this lengthy period of war preparations undoubtedly provides an adversary with quite a few opportunities that it can exploit, by launching a surprise attack or cutting off supply lines, for instance, causing the enemy to collapse without a battle because it is unable to receive supplies in a timely fashion. [authors' translation]

Preemptive strikes may be especially critical to the PLA in the event of the intervention of a powerful third party in a China-Taiwan conflict. According to one Chinese analyst (Lu, 1996), "in military affairs, launching a preemptive strike has always been an effective way in which the party at a disadvantage may overpower its stronger opponent." Lu (1996) argues that launching a preemptive strike would help compensate for China's relative inferiority:

> The paramount mission of a preemptive strike is to neutralize the enemy's high-tech edge and destroy its readiness to launch an attack. That the enemy has more sophisticated weaponry than China is the biggest problem China faces in a future war. Reconnaissance and positioning satellites, AWACS [Airborne Warning and Control System], stealth bombers, aircraft carriers, long-range precision-guided weapons—the enemy has all of that; we don't.[13]

Chinese writers also offer some details about the form preemptive strikes would take. They write that preemptive strikes "should stress sudden attacks of short duration." Some writers suggest that missile strikes and submarines could disrupt the deployment of enemy forces. Others assert that, along with "firepower assaults," electronic warfare, and psychological warfare, SOF would also play a key role in any preemptive strike. SOF units would "infiltrate the enemy's rear area to carry out special operations and sabotage, attacking the critical elements in and key links of its war making machine everywhere—on land, at sea, and in the air" (Lu, 1996). The targets to be attacked would include harbors, airports, transportation links, critical military installations, and C⁴ISR systems.[14]

Engaging in a preemptive strike appears to conflict with the PLA's traditional guideline of striking only after the enemy has struck. Surprisingly, however, preemptive strikes are viewed as consistent with China's "active defense" strategy, as suggested by the following passage from Lu (1996):

> The so-called preemptive strike means taking a series of decisive offensive actions in a battle to attack key targets of the enemy's

---

[13] What is more, the analyst warns, the technological gap between China and its potential adversaries is increasing.

[14] For more on the targets that would be attacked and the approaches the PLA might use to strike them, see Chapter Three.

in-depth campaign formations, diminishing its high-tech edge, impairing its readiness to attack, and creating an advantageous combat situation, all within a strategic framework of gaining mastery by striking only after the enemy has struck.

This paradox is explained by defining the enemy's *first strike* as any "military activities conducted by the enemy aimed at breaking up China territorially and violating its sovereignty" (Lu, 1996). By this definition, any U.S. military support or deployment to address a military crisis around Taiwan could be interpreted as a "military activity aimed at breaking up China" and thereby rendered the equivalent of a "strategic first shot." This could serve as sufficient pretext for China to launch a military strike against U.S. forces (Lu, 1996).

Key-Point Strikes

Chinese writings identify a range of particularly important targets through the concept of 重点打击 ["key-point strikes"]. According to Wang and Zhang (2000, p. 97), the objective of key-point strikes is

> crippling and degrading the enemy's operational superiority. In such a case, one should select the enemy's information systems, command systems, and support systems as targets for concentrated strike. As for ordinary combat adversaries, one should determine targets for concentrated strike based on the objective of annihilating the enemy's effective force strength. [authors' translation]

Or, as one passage puts it, key-point attacks are intended to 先瘫后歼 ["paralyze first and annihilate later"] (Wang and Zhang, 2000, p. 89 [authors' translation]).

The key-point strike concept is based on the premise that all militaries, regardless of how capable or technologically advanced they are, possess areas of vulnerability. Wang and Zhang (2000, p. 96) defines *key points* as targets

> that could have a direct influence on the overall situation of the campaign or produce an overall effect. They include systems,

parts, and links vital to the sustaining of the campaign, as well as important force groupings and important battlefield facilities. [authors' translation]

Wang and Zhang (2000, p. 96) describes this concept as utilizing "flexible and mobile campaign methods" to actively engage "vital targets that integrate and support the enemy's overall operations system."

To launch successful key-point strikes against the enemy's centers of gravity, it is first necessary to identify them. Wang and Zhang (2000, p. 95) lists five types of targets that, if sufficiently degraded or destroyed, could tip the balance in favor of the PLA: 指挥系统 [command systems]; 信息系统 [information systems]; 武器系统 [weapon systems], 后勤系统 [logistics systems]; and, finally, the linkages between these systems [authors' translations].

Command Systems. Command systems are the nerve centers of campaign operations and together with information systems are viewed as the most critical of the five targets (Jiang, 1997, pp. 149–151). Wang and Zhang (2000, p. 95) states that

destroying or crippling the enemy's campaign command system could paralyze the enemy's entire campaign system. Hence, crippling the enemy's command system is vital to the destruction of the overall structure of the enemy's campaign operational system. [authors' translation]

Information Systems. Military information systems comprise complex systems of surveillance and reconnaissance devices, computer equipment, communication facilities, command-and-control facilities, and information processing and display equipment. Chinese strategists view information capabilities as an essential component of a military force's strength. Hence, crippling or destroying the enemy's information system can drastically degrade the enemy's combat capabilities by making it "blind," "deaf," and "paralyzed" (Wang and Zhang, 2000, p. 95).[15]

---

[15] For more information on PLA views on the criticality of information systems, see Mulvenon (1999).

Weapon Systems. According to Wang and Zhang (2000, p. 95), "modern weapon systems are a pillar supporting the entire campaign system. Crippling or destroying the enemy's weapon systems would fundamentally degrade its overall combat capabilities" [authors' translation].

Logistic Systems. Because of their high operational tempos and consumption of materiel, modern campaigns require extensive logistic support. This is more true for the U.S. military than for any other military in the world. According to Wang and Zhang (2000, p. 95), disrupting U.S. logistic support can be an effective way to undermine overall U.S. combat capabilities:

> Modern campaigns, because of their extremely high levels of consumption, depend more and more on logistic and equipment support. Damage inflicted on various bases and on various facilities would also put [a combatant] in a passive position. A lack of fuel, ammunition, supplies, and various technical and support equipment could lead to campaign defeat. The vastness of the battlefield lengthens the logistic and equipment support lines and increases their quantities. Because of the complexity of the technologies involved in weapon systems and the great variety of types of weapon systems, logistic and equipment support cover a large area and many issues and thus have become more difficult. In addition, support systems, most regarded as soft targets and weak in defense, are vulnerable to attack. All these factors have made campaign support systems prime targets of campaign operations. Hence, attacking the enemy's campaign support systems constitutes a vital link in the effort to paralyze the enemy's entire campaign operational structure. [authors' translation][16]

Links Between Systems. Chinese military writers often describe modern war as 系统战 ["a war of systems"]. For these systems to function properly, they must be integrated effectively. As Wang and Zhang (2000, p. 95) explains, "only through close coordination of these [operational] systems can one achieve unified [campaign] objectives"

---

[16] As will be discussed below, Chinese strategists view logistics and support as some of the main potential vulnerabilities of the U.S. military.

[authors' translation]. According to Wang and Zhang (2000, pp. 95–96), it therefore makes sense for the PLA to try to

> sever and cripple the interconnection of the enemy's operational system, command system, weapon system, support system, etc., and the internal links within each system. Destroying their relationship and their coordination would result in the enemy carrying out isolated instead of concerted campaign operations. This would help achieve the objective of degrading the enemy's overall combat capabilities. [authors' translation]

Concentrated Attack

Chinese strategists argue that, once committed to attack, the PLA will need to ensure that the attack employs sufficient force to be effective. Some strategists assert that China will need to use its most advanced platforms as the "core" of the attack (Huang, 1999). As one writer puts it, Chinese military planners must "overcome a mentality of using forces with scrupulous care and should send without hesitation its most advanced technological arms and best picked units to the front" (Huang, 1999). The same article criticizes Iraq's performance in the first Gulf War for firing "Scud missiles like spraying pepper." Huang continues:

> A belligerent should make concentrated use of its advanced technological arms and pick units to a maximum extent and should launch a super-intensive surprise attack within a limited time and limited space, thus putting "overwhelming pressure" on the battlefield and attaining the set goal at one blow.

Another PLA source (Wang and Zhang, 2000, p. 96) describes "concentrated strikes" as

> the concentration of forces along the main axis of the military campaign, at the critical juncture, and for a major operation, with an objective of mounting focused strikes against targets vital to sustaining and supporting the enemy's operational system. Destroying and annihilating such vital targets and quickly para-

lyzing the enemy's operational system should become the focus of campaign execution and the main approach to achieving campaign victory. . . . In directing a campaign, the key to carrying out the concept of concentrated strike is to correctly determine the vital targets for concentrated strike and, at the same time, to concentrate the necessary force to strike at these vital targets. Both are indispensable. [authors' translation]

Achieving Information Superiority

Many Chinese writers regard information collection, processing and transmission and the denial of those capabilities to an adversary as vital to the successful prosecution of a modern high-technology war. Peng and Yao (2001, p. 358) states that

information supremacy is the precondition for achieving supremacy in the air, at sea, and on the ground and is critical to achieving and maintaining battlefield supremacy. Information operations are unavoidably the most important operational method of modern wars. [authors' translation]

As a result of the growing significance of information in conducting high-technology war, "information warfare" has become an increasingly important subject among PLA strategists. Wang and Zhang (2000, p. 169) describes information warfare as

a means, not a goal. The goal of information warfare is, at the critical time and region related to overall campaign operations, to cut off the enemy's ability to obtain, control, and use information and to influence, reduce, and even destroy the enemy's capabilities of observing, decisionmaking, and commanding and controlling troops, while we maintain our own ability to command and control so as to seize information superiority and produce strategic and campaign superiority, creating conditions for winning the decisive battle. [authors' translation]

PLA analysts base many of their judgments about information warfare on observations of how the United States has conducted operations since the first Gulf War. They note that, in the 1990 conflict with Iraq, the first U.S. attacks targeted Iraqi radar sites, and subsequent coalition air strikes were accompanied by large-scale electronic jamming. Examples like these have led many Chinese researchers to conclude that success in modern warfare is no longer a function of the number of casualties inflicted on the enemy or the seizure of territory but of denying information to the enemy. Chen (1998, p. 393) asserts that

> the operational objectives of the two sides on attack and defense are neither the seizing of territory nor the killing of so many enemies, but rather the paralyzing of the other side's information system and the destruction of the other side's will to resist. The enemy's command centers, communication hubs, information processing centers, high-tech weapon control systems, and supply systems could become priority targets of attack. The scenes in the past of close-combat fighting have become history, and where the front and the rear are located is no longer an issue of concern to commanders and units.

The conduct of information warfare also greatly emphasizes the concept of "gaining mastery by striking first." In fact, conducting information operations not only facilitates but may actually require striking first. Specifically, Wang and Zhang (2000, p. 178) states that information operations rely

> more on taking early advantage to seize control over information. This is decided by the characteristics of information warfare. First, an information offensive is mainly launched by remote combat and covert method, making it easier to launch a sudden attack. Second, information warfare consumes fewer human and materiel resources than the conventional combat of forces, so it has stronger sustainability. Once the offensive starts, it can go on incessantly for a long time. Third, information systems operate in the electromagnetic spectrum. Therefore, any operating information system on the battlefield is exposed. Theoretically speaking, it is impossible for an operating information system to completely protect itself from an enemy's information offensive. Moreover,

physical destruction during an information offensive also makes it difficult for the defender to restore the system quickly. These characteristics of information warfare show that whoever takes the early advantage is more likely to seize control over information on the battlefield and achieve a better combat effect. In this sense, active offense requires that, in information warfare on the battlefield, we not only use the offense as our main means but that we also "gain mastery by striking first." [authors' translation; quotation marks in the original]

Key-point attacks are also stressed in information warfare. Of the four important types of campaign operations discussed in Wang and Zhang (2000)—information warfare, combined firepower operations, mobility, and special warfare—attacks against key points are only mentioned in the information warfare section. In fact, Wang and Zhang (2000, p. 179) specifically refers to concentrating

the forces of information offensive at the very beginning of a campaign on directly attacking the vital parts and key links of enemy information systems, destroying enemy information systems first and paralyzing the whole enemy combat system to get the greatest victory with least cost. [authors' translation]

Although gaining information superiority is seen as the key to victory, information superiority does not have to be maintained throughout the entire course of a war and does not need to be achieved in its totality. Rather, information superiority can be seized during specific time periods needed to conduct attacks on vital targets. One source (Dai, 1999, pp. 276–277) states that,

for any strong army, establishing information control is a relative concept, and absolute information control does not exist. For our army, this is even more so. The process of establishing information control is relative, with the scope of control being localized and the gains and losses dynamic. The most important value of information operations is when they are needed by joint operations. The scope of seizure is relative like this, with localized information control increasing effectiveness. [authors' translation]

While information warfare attacks can assume a variety of forms, they generally fall into two main categories: "soft" and "hard" kill methods. Soft-kill methods include computer network attacks and electronic jamming. Some can be carried out clandestinely, are deniable, and often have temporary effects. Hard-kill methods, on the other hand, cause physical destruction and can be carried out through the use of ballistic and cruise missiles, SOF, air strikes, microwave weapons, lasers, particle-beam weapons, and nuclear and nonnuclear electromagnetic pulse (EMP) weapons. The physical destruction that hard kills cause is described as the only method that can thoroughly paralyze information systems and infrastructure (Dai, 1999, p. 272). The targets of these weapons include command personnel, command-and-control facilities, communication centers, computer systems, command-and-control aircraft, and communication satellites.

Raising the Costs of Conflict

In a conflict with the United States, China's strategy must "frustrate the adversary's strategic intentions," undermine its resolve and determination, and prevent it from fighting the type of war it wants to fight. To do so, it is necessary to inflict sufficient casualties and costs for the United States to lose its willingness to continue to engage in the conflict. According to a PLA officer's doctoral dissertation on defeating a superior adversary (Jiang, 1997, pp. 118–119),

> under the conditions of a high-technology local war, when a superpower intervenes directly in the war, it is possible for the side with inferior equipment to strive to gain the initiative on the battlefield and realize its important strategic objectives, control the scale of the war and combine fighting with negotiating, and compel the superior enemy to pull out of the conflict. Because the superpower must cope with the influence of its other fundamental strategic interests, the level of its intervention is limited; moreover, it will seek to win victory in the war at minimum cost. [authors' translation]

This strategy assumes that China can raise the costs of military action to a level the United States deems unacceptable. According to this author (Jiang, 1997, pp. 117–118),

> if we can destroy a portion of the enemy's effective forces, it will create a traumatic experience for the enemy; the resolution to fight the war of an enemy with high-technology equipment that is extremely sensitive to casualties and costs will be clearly shaken; and we will be able to compel the enemy to decide to withdraw from the war. [authors' translation]

As a result, "smashing the adversary's will to resist" has become more important than thoroughly destroying the enemy's military forces in high-technology local wars (Peng and Yao, 2001, pp. 436, 486 [authors' translation]).

This analysis may have worrisome implications if Chinese analysts are convinced that the resolve of China's potential adversaries is relatively weak. Indeed, there is some evidence that Chinese strategists doubt Taiwan's political will to resist Chinese attempts at coercion. For instance, one PLA researcher (Zhu, 2001) asserts that "resolving the Taiwan problem is not a matter of actual strength [实力]; it's a matter of determination [决心]." Some of the same researcher's comments suggest a dangerous overconfidence on the part of at least some in the PLA (Zhu, 2001):

> Apart from the will of the people in Taiwan—practically everyone has a passport from another country—Taiwan's 战斗力 [fighting capacity] is also doubtful. Moreover, there is the tradition of anti-Taiwan independence education, as well as anticommunist education in Taiwan. As soon as the fighting starts, whether the military would support a government that wants Taiwan independence is doubtful. [authors' translation]

Limited Strategic Aims

Chinese strategists recognize that they will not have to achieve a total military victory over the United States. Under conditions of local war, political goals are limited. As a result, China need only achieve a relative military victory to attain its larger political objectives. As one Chinese source (Jiang, 1997, pp. 115–117) notes,

> since the end of the Second World War, in the majority of wars in which the side with inferior equipment has defeated an enemy with superior equipment, the inferior side has won a relative military victory, compelling the superior enemy to stop fighting or to retreat from the battlefield. [authors' translation]

This has been the case for two primary reasons. The first is that the relative imbalance between the weapons and capabilities of the two sides in a conflict has "limited the scale, scope, and level of the victory" won by the inferior side, making it impossible for that side to seek a further expansion of its gains. The second is that the superior adversary in such conflicts has usually had limited strategic objectives. Consequently, "once the technologically superior enemy calculates that the risks and cost of the war are becoming too great, it often will give up on trying to use military actions to achieve its political objectives" (Jiang, 1997, p. 116 [authors' translation]).

Thus, in a high-technology local war that pits a relatively inferior country against a superior adversary, China need not seek a purely military victory. Instead, it can achieve its objectives through a combination of "partial military victory on the battlefield plus ultimate political victory at the negotiating table" (Jiang, 1997 [authors' translation]). This may require it to fight and negotiate at the same time and to use military pressure to gain an advantage in negotiations, especially if negotiations become complicated and protracted.[17] The objective of such force is to position China to end the conflict on terms that are as advantageous as possible.

The principal challenges the PLA must confront are preventing the United States from prevailing in an initial engagement, controlling any subsequent escalation, and creating an environment in which it holds a strong advantage in negotiations (Jiang, 1997, pp. 116–117).

---

[17] This tactic is certainly not new for the PRC, which employed it during the Korean War and other conflicts.

Modern Military Capabilities

It is important to note that the principles described above are considered complements to, not substitutes for, military modernization and the acquisition of high-technology weapon systems. For example, in a discussion of China's relative deficiencies in long-range precision-strike capabilities, Wang and Zhang (2000, p. 25) recommend that China both acquire new capabilities to launch and defend against such attacks and, in the meantime, devise approaches that make it possible to carry out and counter such attacks using current capabilities:

> In the face of this serious challenge in the development of future campaign trends, [the PLA] must strive to enhance its deep and multidimensional campaign operations to new heights. That is, it must possess certain capabilities to mount deep and multi-dimensional strikes, and at the same time, it must also have fairly good protective capabilities to effectively counter deep and multi-dimensional strikes mounted by the enemy. This requires that, on the one hand, it improve its weapon systems and equipment and explore new combat methods and that, on the other hand, based on present conditions, it search for ways and means, with characteristics of its own, to mount or counter in-depth and multidimensional strikes. [authors' translation]

PLA authors point out that the Chinese military already has some sophisticated weapons of its own, including some that are at or near world-class levels. "Under modern conditions," one PLA officer (Jiang, 1997, p. 114) writes,

> the shortcomings of the weapons and equipment of the Chinese military are relative; 劣中有优 [there is some superiority amidst inferiority]; and there are ways to improve and make up for [the weaknesses]. [authors' translation]

Chinese Perceptions of U.S. Vulnerabilities

Chinese security analysts assess that the United States has a number of important military and strategic vulnerabilities that should be targeted in the event of conflict. Perhaps no potential U.S. military vulnerability is as important, in Chinese eyes, as its heavy reliance on its information, or C[4]ISR, network (Dai, 2002). Chinese strategists believe that the U.S. military's awesome power derives in large degree from its effective integration and use of information technology. More so than the capabilities of individual platforms, such as fighters or aircraft carriers, it is its C[4]ISR system that gives the United States capabilities so far beyond those of other countries. Effectively attacking that system will affect U.S. combat capabilities much more profoundly than would directly targeting combat platforms. As one writer from the Chinese Academy of Military Science argues, "if they [the United States] fail to acquire or transmit information, digital forces will be paralyzed, their combat capability would shrink rapidly, and they will lose the initiative on the battlefield" (Lu, 1996). The U.S. C[4]ISR system represents its "military nerve center," and damaging it may throw the enemy into disarray, turning it into a "group without a leader" (Jiang, 1997, pp. 149–150 [authors' translation]).

Chinese strategists also believe the U.S. military information network to be both fragile and vulnerable (Dai, 2002). A number of Chinese writers argue that the high-technology systems that form the backbone of the U.S. C[4]ISR network are fragile and susceptible to both hard and soft attacks. Networks as large and complex as the one the U.S. military uses are said to be inherently unreliable and open to disruption (Jiang, 1997, pp. 151–152). Thus, the foundation of the U.S. military's success can also be its undoing.

Chinese analysts argue that another problem the United States confronts is that it will have difficulty establishing a position of clear military superiority at the outset of a conflict if hostilities begin before its forces are fully deployed.

An assessment of the United States' experience in the Gulf War offered in one Chinese book highlights the challenges the United States encounters when deploying its forces to distant regions across the globe. During the Gulf War, the author writes, it took only about 14 hours for U.S. aircraft to travel from the continental United States to the region, but it took 14 days for many ships to reach the Persian Gulf. The total time required for preparation was five months, more than long enough for Iraq to have taken some sort of action to disrupt the U.S. deployment to the theater, had Baghdad decided to launch a preemptive strike (Li, 1995, pp. 189–190).

Closely related to the challenges of rapid deployment are issues of logistics and supply. When U.S. forces operate at great distances, supply lines are long, and ensuring effective logistics support is extremely challenging, according to Chinese analysts. One Chinese author writes that U.S. combat forces deploy with very limited supplies, perhaps enough to last for no more than two to five days (Li, 1995, pp. 189–190).[18] Thus, the logistics and support requirements of high-technology forces are seen as particularly daunting. For example, Chinese military writers estimate that an aircraft carrier strike group requires replenishment of 60,000 tons of 一般燃料 ["ordinary fuel"] and 30,000 tons of aviation fuel every four to five days (Jiang, 1997, pp. 113–114 [authors' translation]). This forces the United States to scramble to mount complex logistics and support operations. Chinese analysts estimate that it can take as much as three to four months for the United States to establish a complete logistics and supply network in a distant theater of operations (Li, 1995, pp. 189–190).[19]

Chinese analysts also note that the United States possesses several key strategic weaknesses (see Pan and Sun, 1994, pp. 236–238). The first and, according to some Chinese writers, most important of these is the extraordinary difficulties the United States would confront if it found itself engaged in two high-technology local wars at the same time. A number of Chinese analysts have argued that this problem was brought into sharp relief by the extent of the U.S. commitment in Kosovo.[20] Some argued that the U.S. intervention there was emblematic of a pattern of U.S. military overcommitment, with

---

[18] The author estimates that an Army division deploys with three to five days of supplies and that an Army brigade carries enough supplies to last two to three days.

[19] The actual time required would of course depend on the scale and location of the operation.

[20] See, for example, Tang (1999). Much of this article, published in the semimonthly of the Shanghai Institute of International Studies, appears to be highly derivative of the analysis presented in Pan and Sun (1994, pp. 236–238); see also Wei and Li (2000). The article reports on interviews with several Chinese Academy of Military Science researchers, includ-

the result that limited military resources were being spread too thinly across too many regions. This view was encapsulated in an article published in the China Institute for International Studies journal. Yang (1999) asserted that the United States was beginning to suffer from imperial overreach:

> The Kosovo crisis has exposed again the conflict between the US strategic intention of global domination and its limited might. While U.S. military might is unmatched, since the end of the Cold War, due to frequent foreign interventions, U.S. military might is showing signs of being "overused," with its personnel and equipment both being in short supply.

The article concluded that the crisis revealed the erosion of the U.S. military's capability to handle two conflicts simultaneously. In the words of the author, "That small Kosovo war was too much for the United States to cope with, putting into question the U.S. military strategy of simultaneously winning two regional conflicts" (Yang, 1999). As a result of this increasing tendency toward imperial overreach, according to Pan and Sun (1994, p. 237), "America worries that, once its military is drawn into a conflict in some region, a regional power in a second or third area might take advantage of the occasion to provoke another war, making it difficult for America to respond" [authors' translation]. Chinese analysts regard assertions that the United States could fight two regional wars at the same time as an attempt to placate allies that belies the inability of the United States to prosecute two conflicts simultaneously.[21]

Chinese writers argue that a second problem with U.S. strategy is that U.S. leaders must confront several domestic factors—chief among them partisan politics, potential public opposition, a highly critical media, and an assertive Congress—that restrict their military and dip-

---

ing Min Zhenfan, Wang Zhenxi, Fan Gaoyue, and Yao Yunzhu, as well as Wang Liqun of the PLA Air Force Command Academy.

[21] Although, with its recent operations in Iraq, the United States has certainly showed that it can sustain a much higher level of military effort than was involved in Kosovo, these analysts would probably now argue that the United States would be hard pressed to prosecute a second conflict as long as it remains involved in Iraq.

lomatic options. Chinese writers frequently argue that these domestic pressures are functions of an almost total unwillingness on the part of U.S. leaders and the American public to accept casualties in contemporary military conflicts. One *Liberation Army Daily* article, for example, asserts that the U.S. public is "abnormally sensitive" about military casualties and that its tolerance for casualties is continuing to decline. "Once casualties occur in a war," the author asserts, "a domestic antiwar cry arises" (Du, 2000). Another analyst similarly asserts that the United States has a very limited capacity to withstand personnel casualties and is concerned that casualties will give rise to domestic antiwar sentiment (Li, 1995, p. 190).[22] Chinese analysts assess that even a small number of casualties is sufficient to spark strong popular opposition and erode domestic support for U.S. participation in a conflict. The U.S. experience in Somalia is usually cited in support of this assertion.[23] In addition, Chinese analysts argue that this lack of resolve on the part of the United States was demonstrated again in the Kosovo intervention. According to one Chinese analyst, the Clinton administration's reluctance to consider the use of ground forces in the Kosovo conflict "showed that the United States is unwilling to pay too great a price for its foreign interventions" (Yang, 1999).

A third major weakness in U.S. strategy, in the view of PLA strategists, and of most significance for this study, is America's "heavy reliance" on assistance from its allies, including everything from political and financial support to basing and overflight rights. The United States cannot successfully carry out major military operations without significant assistance from its allies and cooperation from other countries, according to Chinese analysts. According to Yang (1999),

> when the United States carries out a local war, not only does it need political and diplomatic support from its allies, it is even

---

[22] This may limit U.S. military options, according to the author.

[23] See, for example, Tang (1999). According to Tang,

> after entering Somalia, the people in the United States showed strong reaction when 18 Rangers were killed in a battle. This forced the U.S. military to give up its goal in Somalia, [resulting in] the end [to] all military activities there, and the withdrawal of all invading troops in dejection.

more dependent on their economic assistance and military participation.

Many Chinese strategists argue that the United States would not have been able to win the Gulf War without the assistance and support of its coalition partners. According to one analyst, the heavy U.S. reliance on allies was one of the major problems PLA theoreticians identified in their studies of the Gulf War (Li, 1995, p. 188). In addition, some Chinese writers assess that U.S. reliance on allies was even more pronounced in the Kosovo conflict (Tang, 1999).[24] The conclusion PLA strategists reached is that the U.S. military will need to rely on the assistance of allies and friends to prevail in future conflicts and that this will likely cause operational and political problems for the United States.

The most critical aspect of this dependence on allied support is the requirement for access to forward bases, which is seen as a major limitation on the effectiveness of U.S. responses to regional crises. As one Chinese analyst writes in an article published in an official journal (Jiang, 1999),

> forward bases are indispensable for . . . U.S. joint operations. A case in point is the dependence of air force units on forward bases in launching . . . operations against ground and naval forces. They directly affect the intensity and continuity of the . . . operations through such key factors as sortie and replenishment rates. Due to the great reduction of permanent overseas U.S. military bases after the Cold War and the fact that regional crises tend to break out quite suddenly, U.S. forces often find themselves lacking forward bases.

The U.S. style of war is so dependent on access to forward bases, the author continues, that without access to "first-line" forward bases, U.S. forces "will have difficulty launching multiple waves of quick and sudden air strikes." If they are forced to rely solely on "second- and

---

[24] After discussing the military and financial assistance provided by U.S. allies in the Gulf War, Tang (1999) asserts that "The US dependence on allies was even more conspicuous in the Kosovo War."

third-line airfields" and aircraft carriers to launch air strikes, their overall operational capabilities "will be greatly diminished" (Jiang Chuan, 1999). Chinese analysts note that the U.S. bases on Okinawa would play a critical role in any U.S. response to a crisis on the Korean peninsula or in the Taiwan Strait. In particular, they emphasize the crucial role of U.S. fighter aircraft and ASW aircraft stationed on Okinawa, in responding to a Taiwan crisis (Kang, 1998). Chinese sources have also noted local displays of resentment over the continued presence of U.S. forces on Okinawa and the tensions these incidents have caused between Washington and Tokyo.[25]

This perceived U.S. reliance on allies for basing and support is seen as a weakness for several reasons. For example, PLA analysts from AMS note that the United States encountered numerous problems— from interoperability and coordination to political disputes within the coalition—in cooperating with its allies in the Kosovo war. The conflict highlighted the political difficulties of alliance warfare because "the extent to which military action is affected and restricted by political factors increases as the scale of the alliance expands" (see Wei and Li, 2000). Disagreements within NATO and domestic political pressures in some alliance countries all restricted the military options available to the United States in the conflict. According to Li (1995, p. 189), these weaknesses are ones that adversaries of the United States will be able to exploit in future conflicts:

> In alliance warfare, there are differences in interests, military strategy, weapons and equipment, culture, and language among the militaries of the various countries, and there will be problems of command and coordination. This can provide an adversary with an 可乘之机 [opportunity that can be exploited] by splitting and causing collapse [of the enemy's alliances] politically and by routing [the enemy] militarily. [authors' translation]

---

[25] See, for example, Zhang and Yi (2000) and Liu Lisheng (2000).

CHAPTER THREE

Elements of Chinese Military Strategy with Potential Implications for U.S. Theater Access

As noted at the beginning of the previous chapter, we found no explicit use of the term "antiaccess" in Chinese military writings. This is probably because Chinese strategists do not consider an antiaccess strategy by itself to be sufficient to prevent or defeat a militarily superior power. The writings we reviewed nonetheless suggest that key elements of a comprehensive Chinese strategy for defeating a military power like the United States would consist of actions designed to impede U.S. military access to the Asian theater in the event of a U.S.-China conflict. These include attacking U.S. C⁴ISR systems; attacking logistics, transportation, and support functions; attacking air bases; blockading and attacking sea lanes and ports; attacking aircraft carriers; and preventing the use of bases on allied territory.[1]

Attacks on C⁴ISR Systems

As noted above, Chinese strategists view the U.S. information network as one of its most vital key points to target because disrupting U.S. communications and critical command-and-control centers would leave the affected U.S. forces in a "state of paralysis" (Jiang, 1997, pp. 113–114 [authors' translation]). Attacks on C⁴ISR targets could

---

[1] It is important to bear in mind, however, that these antiaccess elements are embedded within the context of a larger strategy designed to counter technologically advanced military powers, such as the United States, and are not a distinct strategy in and of themselves.

have an antiaccess effect by disrupting the deployment of U.S. military forces to a region or by interfering with command, control, and communication or early warning capabilities to the extent that a decision would be made to withdraw forward-deployed forces farther from the locus of conflict.

Attacks against C⁴ISR systems can involve operations against military and civilian targets in all five dimensions—land, sea, air, space, and cyberspace—and can be undertaken during peacetime and wartime. As described earlier, Chinese strategists argue that the more a military relies on information technology, the more vulnerable it becomes to information attacks. In what the Chinese would describe as a "contradiction," the strength of the U.S. military is hinged on the successful use of information. This strength, however, is also seen as being its weakness.

Chinese writings describe a combination of soft- and hard-kill methods for defeating an enemy's C⁴ISR system. Dong et al. (1999, p. 107) recognizes, however, that purely soft methods are unlikely to be sufficient to achieve overall victory in a campaign, noting that it will be

> difficult for [electronic warfare] to form an independent campaign stage or an independent campaign. It can form a type of independent method, but in order to achieve a complete campaign victory, firepower strikes will need to be relied upon. [authors' translation]

Another author writes that "every type of campaign method" should be used to defeat an enemy's C⁴ISR system (Dai, 1999, p. 273 [authors' translation]). To illustrate how a combination of hard- and soft-kill methods can best be carried out, Dai (1999, pp. 303–304) describes how a battle against command-and-control systems might develop:

> The first attack wave should come as early as possible. In reality, early in the preparation stages for war and during the deterrence stages before a war, the first wave is already being conducted in the invisible information space. This attack consists mainly of

intelligence warfare, psychological warfare, military deception, and military deterrence or is conducted in conjunction with a political and diplomatic battle. Adopted measures include psychological deception, electronic deception, and network (semantic meaning) [sic] attack. The main goals are to collect intelligence from enemy information systems and networks and to conduct scattered and concealed information harassment and attacks in conjunction with military and diplomatic efforts to conceal our operational intent. The first wave is actually only the preparation or prologue to seizing campaign information superiority.

After the stage of seizing campaign information superiority, the first round of attacks are concentrated, complete, and focused information suppression attacks using electromagnetic suppression, powerful electronic warfare attack, and computer network countermeasures to carry out concentrated interference, suppression, and destruction attacks against the enemy's strategic and campaign-level information systems. The primary targets are the hearts and minds of the enemy's information handling and decisionmaking centers, as well as those of the operational systems' eyes and ears, such as information monitoring resources and the nerve centers of information lines, to greatly reduce the information system's capability and to create beneficial conditions for subsequent firepower attacks. Effective concentrated information suppression relies on large-scale and direct suppression and powerful destructive attacks against the enemy's campaign- and strategic-level information systems. When information attacks are not strong enough, joint firepower attacks can be directly carried out, and multiple types of firepower attacks and special operations can make up for a lack in information attacks.

After the second wave of attacks effectively weakens and suppresses the enemy's information systems, especially command-and-control centers, the enemy's radars will be blind, communications broken, command paralyzed, and coordination lost. Weapons will be out of control and temporarily blind and deaf or even paralyzed. The opportunity should not be missed to organize missile attacks against information nodes. Cruise missiles and stealth aircraft can conduct pinpoint strikes against the enemy's command-and-control centers, air-defense systems, electronic warfare centers, ground-to-ground missile bases, and other point targets. Tactical ballistic missiles can also strike targets throughout a country. When missiles are launched, air- and sea-based electronic interference will be used against the electronic systems of strategic warning and missile defense systems. During missile penetrations, missile penetration electronic countermeasure devices will be used to interfere with and deceive the enemy's missile defense system and carry out necessary tactical maneuvers. At the same time as firepower attacks are being conducted, electronic interference, computer virus, antiradiation, and directed-energy weapon attacks should be conducted against electronic information systems, especially command-and-control centers and nodes to form a combination of "soft" and "hard" attacks. Special attention must be paid to destroying and suppressing the enemy's air-defense system to create conditions for strikes by the air force. [authors' translation]

This passage does not necessarily represent official doctrine (particularly since China does not currently possess such systems as stealth aircraft), and most writings speak about attacking C⁴ISR systems in general and do not prioritize targets or methods. Examples like this one do, however, illustrate how far Chinese researchers have thought through the use of information operations. Moreover, several information warfare methods—computer network attacks, EMP attacks, and attacks against satellites—have particular implications for U.S. theater access.

Computer Network Attacks

Computer network attacks receive special attention as "one of the most effective ways for weak militaries to fight strong militaries" (Wang and Zhang, 2000, p. 174 [authors' translation]). In fact, some Chinese strategists believe them to be so effective that an "entire coordinated and unified command and control capability can be lost" (Dai, 1999, p. 234 [authors' translation]). These sources describe various types of computer network attack methods, including hacker attacks, virus attacks, information pollution, information harassment, and surveillance methods.

Attacks can be conducted remotely via computers or, ideally, at the target site by infiltrators (Lu, 1999, p. 320). Chinese strategists claim that computer network attacks are likely to have a high degree of success in disrupting U.S. military operations, in part because military information systems are connected to commercial lines. One source (Lu, 1999, p. 311), for example, recommends utilizing

> a computer network's geographic scope, many customers, and high degree of resource-sharing to enter international networks, civil-military networks and communications equipment to carry out virus destruction. It has been divulged that in the United States 95 percent of military networks pass through civilian lines and that 150,000 military computers pass through normal computer networks. This characteristic of computer networks makes it easy to conduct virus attack. [authors' translation]

According to this same source, hackers attempted to infiltrate U.S. military computer systems more than 250,000 times in 1995, with a success rate of 65 percent (Lu, 1999, p. 305). For example, Chinese authors assert that, during the Kosovo conflict, Yugoslavian hackers attacked the command-and-control system of a U.S. aircraft carrier, temporarily degrading its performance (Peng and Yao, 2001, pp. 363–364).

Operations against computer networks are not limited to wartime. Peacetime operations against computer networks include computer reconnaissance methods that infiltrate computer systems to obtain intelligence or to reconnoiter computer systems for weaknesses that can be exploited during wartime. Other methods involve infiltrating computer systems to render command-and-control systems dysfunctional. One example given of "winning without fighting" is inserting a virus into an enemy's nuclear weapon command-and-control computer system during peacetime to alter its code and render it unusable (Lu, 1999, p. 308). Infiltration of computer systems is described as being used against the Iraqi army before the Gulf War in 1991. According to one author, the United States placed infected computer chips in French-made antiaircraft computer components destined for Iraq. When these components were installed into the Iraqi air-defense system, the virus spread throughout the system and "rendered critical Iraqi weapon command-and-control systems useless and caused immeasurable damage" (Lu, 1999, p. 309 [authors' translation]).

Chinese discussions of computer network operations appear to include the possibility of attacking DoD computer systems in the United States. In this regard, information operations enable the PLA to exert a form of long-range power projection to attack a variety of targets. While the vulnerability of the U.S. military to these sorts of attacks may be debatable, that the Chinese have identified command-and-control as the U.S. center of gravity suggests that these types of targets will be a focus of Chinese attacks.

EMP Attacks

A number of Chinese writers suggest utilizing EMP weapons to disrupt the U.S. C4ISR system. One Chinese source (Dai, 1999, p. 272) describes EMP attacks as including

> nuclear EMP attacks and nonnuclear EMP attacks. Nuclear and thermonuclear explosions create a large EMP effect that can cause electronic equipment to be overloaded and ruined. This type of large nuclear EMP can cause electronic systems within hundreds to over a thousand kilometers to be destroyed. The effective power of a nonnuclear EMP burst is several million times greater than those of current jammers (reaching 10,000 MW) and can burn unprotected and highly sensitive and even complete electronic equipment (systems) [sic], as well as destroy the normal operation of computer systems. [authors' translation]

Another source (Nie, 1999, p. 185) speaks of using EMP weapons as part of an attack on an aircraft carrier strike group:

> We can use the Second Artillery or the Air Force to deliver an EMP bomb to the enemy's large naval force to destroy the enemy's warning and detection systems, operational command sys-

tems, and other electronic information systems. [authors' translation][2]

Attacks on Satellites

Space warfare, a subset of information warfare, is also receiving an increasing amount of attention from Chinese military writers. The U.S. military's use of space for strategic reconnaissance, communications, navigation and positioning, and early warning have highlighted the importance of space as a force multiplier. In part because of these observations, Chinese writers have predicted that space power will develop as airpower has developed, from a reconnaissance force into a strategic bombing force. Because of this, space is thought to be the next "strategic vantage point" from which the control of the air, land, and sea will be determined. According to this logic, the importance of seizing control in space in future battles makes space warfare inevitable. PLA strategists envision the possible expansion of electronic warfare into outer space in future conflicts (Peng and Yao, 2001, p. 363):

> As a result of the continuous development of space technology, military satellites will provide increasingly powerful command-and-control capabilities in future wars. Thus, it is possible that military satellites will become targets for attack in electronic warfare and that space electronic warfare will become a new field of electronic warfare. [authors' translation]

Moreover, many PLA writers have concluded that U.S. space-based systems are vulnerable to attack. A *Liberation Army Daily* article (Li and Chen, 2001, p. 17) states that

---

[2] It is unclear whether the author quoted is talking about a nuclear or nonnuclear EMP, although one suspects that, if he were talking about nuclear EMP, he would have said, "We can use the Second Artillery or Air Force to deliver an EMP attack using a nuclear bomb" rather than "deliver an EMP bomb." According to an article in *Aerospace Power Chronicles*, the effective radius of a nonnuclear EMP weapon would be "on the order of hundreds of meters" (Kopp, 1996), which would be enough to upset or damage the electronics on an individual ship but not an entire formation of ships.

space systems have increasingly become systems in which countries' key interests lie. If an anti-satellite weapon destroys a space system in a future war, the destruction will have dealt a blow to the side that owns and uses the space system, stripped it of space supremacy, and weakened its supremacy in conducting information warfare, and even its supremacy in the war at large. Anti-satellite weapons that can be developed at low cost and that can strike at the enemy's enormously expensive yet vulnerable space system will become an important option for the majority of medium-sized and small countries with fragile space technology.

A Xinhua article reiterates this sentiment: "For countries that can never win a war with the United States by using the method of tanks and planes, attacking the U.S. space system may be an irresistible and most tempting choice" (Wang Hucheng, 2000). Moreover, one PLA source states that during the Gulf War, 90 percent of strategic communications were handled by satellites, including commercial satellites (Dai, 1999, p. 350). Successfully attacking U.S. space-based communication systems would thus have a powerful effect on the ability of the United States to communicate with forces in a given theater of operations.

Satellites can be attacked using both soft- and hard-kill methods. Jamming is an example of a soft-kill method, while hard-kill methods include a whole range of antisatellite technology, including missiles, directed-energy weapons, and antisatellite satellites. Chinese writings on antisatellite operations are generally circumspect, especially in relation to hard kills; however, while no one method is valued more than another, these writings suggest a desire to develop antisatellite weapons. Moreover, one article notes that, although China's aerospace industry has built a solid foundation, "it is still far from meeting the requirements for winning a local war under high-technology conditions" (Xie, Qin, and Huang, 2002). The article further states that

In the future, space military systems will directly participate in local wars that break out around our periphery, including space information support and even offensive and defensive countermeasures. In facing this threat, we should concentrate on intensifying research into the crucial technologies of land-based and space-based (concentrating on space-based) antisatellite weapons and, as soon as possible, develop one or two antisatellite weapons that can threaten the enemy's space systems and seize the initiative in future space wars. [authors' translation]

While Chinese writers do discuss attacking satellites, we found no direct evidence about what types of space targets the PLA may consider the most important. Chinese authors do not assign a relative value to satellites and instead list all types of satellites as potential targets. Chinese sources on strategy and information warfare, however, provide some clues as to what types of targets may be considered most valuable. As detailed earlier (see pp. 35–37), Wang and Zhang (2000) lists five key types of targets. If these types are presented in order of importance, Chinese strategy would seem to value the destruction of intelligence-gathering satellites, which would belong to the second category—information systems—over other types of satellites, such as communication and Global Positioning System satellites, which provide links between various campaign systems and therefore fall into the fifth category.

This prioritization is supported by various writings on information warfare. In these, information collection is regarded as the basis of information warfare. One source states that "the direct goal and basis of operations to achieve campaign information control is the collection of information and the maintaining of information superiority" (Zhang, 1999, p. 68 [authors' translation]). In fact, one source describes 情报战 ["intelligence warfare"] as the primary operational method and asserts that whoever achieves intelligence superiority will then be able to achieve a high degree of battlefield transparency, which can then lead to seizing operational initiative and winning the war (Lu, 1999, p. 74). Another source (Xu, 1999, p. 29) goes further by describing intelligence warfare as holding a special position in the realm of information countermeasures:

"Know the enemy and know yourself, and you can fight a hundred battles without defeat." Under information warfare conditions, only by having clear intelligence on the enemy and the operational area and even the enemy's country, and by strictly controlling our intelligence, can correct judgments of the battle-field be made, correct operational guidance given, and information attacks and firepower attacks correctly organized to para-lyze enemy operational systems and maintain the concealment of operational movement to accomplish campaign goals. [authors' translation]

Perhaps because intelligence collection forms the basis of information superiority, one source states that "before an operation, or in the opening stages of an operation, enemy reconnaissance and early warning systems must be struck" (Xu, 1999, p. 29 [authors' translation]). This statement is echoed in Dai (1999, p. 313), which states that

when a campaign starts, the main tasks of an information operation are to attack enemy reconnaissance systems and implement campaign information deception to conceal our operational intent and protect the start of our campaign force. [authors' translation]

Attacks on Logistics, Transportation, and Support Functions

Launching attacks against the enemy's logistics system is another key element of China's overall strategy for dealing with the U.S. military that has antiaccess implications. Chinese military writings discuss launching attacks on logistics, transportation, and support facilities. The goals of these kinds of attacks would be to delay the deployment of new U.S. forces to the region and render existing forces in the region less effective or more vulnerable because of a lack of timely supplies of materiel needed for warfighting.

PLA authors frequently note that an enemy with high-technology equipment has a high rate of consumption on the battlefield, which translates into heavy requirements for logistics support. As noted above, PLA authors have written that the high level of consumption in modern high-technology campaigns makes the U.S. heavily dependent on complex logistics and support, and this is seen as one of the main vulnerabilities of U.S. forces. Striking a high-technology enemy's logistics system and interdicting its logistics and transportation are thus seen as means of making it difficult for the high-technology enemy to sustain its combat operations (Jiang, 1997, pp. 149–150).

Internal Chinese military writings stress the importance of attacks on logistics and rear-area support in many types of modern high-technology campaigns. One source notes that "Modern campaign systems . . . increasingly rely on the rear area" (Zhan, 1997, p. 348 [authors' translation]). Military forces rely on oil, supplies, ammunition, and other items, and the lack of these can lead to defeat. They also depend on many types of bases and installations and, if these were destroyed, the effect on the forces would be crippling. For example, destroying a road or bridge "would paralyze transportation." Support systems are seen as soft and therefore "prime targets." As one author puts it, the "long supply lines and large [support] structure" of the enemy are "soft targets that are relatively easy to attack." In all, according to this source, "destroying the rear area is an important part of destroying the complete structure" (Zhan, 1997, p. 104 [authors' translation]).

This emphasis on attacking logistics, transportation, and support capabilities is echoed by another source, which indicates that a major operational goal is to 破坏敌保障系统 ["cripple the enemy's support systems"] (Wang and Zhang, 2000, pp. 95–96 [authors' translation]). High-technology militaries are extremely dependent on logistics and support, and attacks against these targets could severely complicate or disrupt their combat operations. In another passage, Wang and Zhang (2000, p. 351) stresses that a key goal for PLA planners is

> to disrupt the enemy's campaign depth or rear area railway and highway hubs, ports, bridges, and other transport systems and logistic supply networks, to block or slow its heavy troop concentration, and to cut off its supplies so as to isolate it from the battlefield. [authors' translation]

Ballistic missiles, cruise missiles, aircraft, SOF, saboteurs, and computer network attack would all be used to degrade an adversary's transportation, logistics, and support capabilities. Some sources suggest that SOF might play a particularly important role in attacking logistics and support targets. According to PLA authors, the enemy's storage facilities, fuel storage bases, and supply depots are especially vulnerable to missile strikes, air attack, and sabotage (Jiang, 1997, pp. 150–151). In addition, aerial-refueling aircraft, transport ships, freighters, railways, roads, and bridges are also identified as targets in Chinese writings.

Attacks on Enemy Air Bases

Another military strategy with antiaccess implications that Chinese writers have identified is attacking enemy air bases to disrupt and degrade enemy air operations. PLA Air Force doctrine envisions that enemy air bases, along with command-and-control facilities and surface-to-air missile (SAM) sites, would be the main targets of initial strikes early in a campaign (Stokes, 2001, p. 45). According to one source, attacking enemy air bases can quickly degrade an adversary's offensive capabilities. For this reason, "It is the most effective way of seizing air superiority" (Zhan, 1997, p. 310 [authors' translation]).

Chinese sources, however, appear to recognize the difficulties inherent in successfully attacking air bases. As Wang and Zhang (2000, p. 362) notes,

> mounting counterattacks against the air bases housing the enemy assault force and weapons is an extremely complex operation. One should meticulously organize coordination among various participating forces and various supporting forces, accurately seize combat opportunities, strive to fight battles of quick resolution, launch swift strikes, and swiftly disengage, so as to win great victories at small cost. Once the mission is completed, one should swiftly divert one's own forces and guard vigilantly against enemy retaliation. [authors' translation]

Writings reviewed in this study suggest that runways, high-value aircraft, critical installations, and support facilities, as well as aircraft crews and support personnel, are all seen as vital targets in attacks on air bases.[3] Wang and Zhang (2000, p. 362) observes that,

> if an attack is aimed at disrupting the enemy air strike plans, one should target the enemy's command-and-control systems and fuel and ammunition supply systems; if it is aimed at degrading an enemy aviation corps group to reduce the pressures from its air strikes, one should target the aircraft parked on the tarmacs of airports housing the enemy's main bomber and fighter-bomber aviation corps. [authors' translation]

Chinese strategists discuss attacking enemy airfields using a range of methods, including ballistic missiles, cruise missiles, fighters and bombers armed with precision-guided munitions, SOF, and covert operatives. These operations might be conducted either together or separately. Conventional ballistic missiles are seen as especially effective in attacks on large-scale fixed targets, such as air bases.[4] Launching missile attacks against enemy air bases is thus regarded as "one of the most important counter-air strike measures" (Cui, 2002, p. 214 [authors' translation]).

In addition to missile and air strikes, Chinese sources indicate that covert operatives, such as SOF or saboteurs, would also play an important role in attacks on enemy air bases. Some writings on the general missions that are assigned to SOF units suggest their role in air base attacks would include strategic reconnaissance, harassment attacks, and direct-action missions, such as carrying out strikes on critical base facilities, destroying aircraft, and assassinating key personnel.[5]

---

[3] See, for example, Zhan (1997, p. 310). According to this source, strikes against enemy air bases would involve a combination of air forces and short-range ballistic missiles. The attacks should be "concentrated and unexpected." This book argues that the attack should be sequenced so that the first strikes damage enemy runways to prevent takeoffs and landings, with subsequent strikes destroying aircraft on the ground.

[4] See Cui (2002, pp. 40, 176). Cui argues that the long-range strike capabilities of conventional missile units allow them to "effectively suppress the other side's air bases," as well as air defense assets and other targets [authors' translation].

[5] For more on the roles of Chinese SOF in campaigns, see Wang and Zhang (2000, pp. 213–220). For a source that provides a brief organizational history of Chinese SOF, see Qu, Liu, and Shi (2000).

None of the writings we reviewed explicitly discussed specific U.S. air bases in the theater or elsewhere that should be attacked. In most cases, the sources are probably referring to options for attacks against air bases in Taiwan. As one U.S. analyst notes, however, PLA authors have stated that China would reserve the right to attack enemy targets on the territory of a third country if that country allowed the enemy to use the bases on its territory in a conflict with China (see Stokes, 2001, p. 38).[6] One *Liberation Army Daily* writer observes that the United States tends to use bases in "third countries' territory" when conducting military operations. The writer goes on to assert that, when a third country allows the United States to use its bases, it immediately loses its neutral status in the conflict. Huang (1999) concludes that, thus,

> a country subject to aggression or armed intervention not only has the right to attack the enemy's combat forces and arms deployed on the enemy's territory and the high seas but also has a totally legitimate reason to attack the enemy targets on the third country's territory.

In addition, Second Artillery (China's missile forces) officers have suggested that there would be opportunities to launch missile strikes against the air force of an "intervening superpower" in a Taiwan conflict (Stokes, 2001, p. 65).

Blockades

Blockades have the potential to deny, disrupt, degrade, or otherwise complicate the arrival of U.S. forces and supplies in a region via sea.[7] Chinese writings reveal the potential these types of operations are believed to have for achieving both political and military objectives. Chinese writings on blockades often overlap with writings on attacks on sea lanes and ports (discussed in the following section) because these actions are often conducted simultaneously.

---

[6]   The warning appeared in Huang (1999).

[7]   For an additional discussion of this topic, see Goldstein and Murray (2004, pp. 161–196, especially pp. 187–194).

Wang and Zhang (2000, p. 407) defines a *blockade campaign* as

> an offensive campaign undertaken to impose a sea or aerial blockade on an enemy entrenched on islands. A large-scale island blockade campaign is often under the unified command of a combined campaign commander and commanding organ, with naval, air force, and Second Artillery campaign force corps as the main campaign force, supported by army, armed police units, and militias. A small-scale blockade campaign is, in general, undertaken by a naval campaign corps in coordination with other services and arms. [authors' translation]

Blockades accomplish campaign objectives by coercing opponents, by undermining the enemy's will to fight and its war-making potential, and by isolating the opponent (Wang and Zhang, 2000, p. 409).

The multidimensional nature of blockades presents challenges in that a total blockade of an area would mean preventing aircraft, surface ships, and submarines from entering it. This would require joint operations involving all military services with the assistance of civilians. Wang and Zhang (2000, p. 411) states that blockades should, first,

> bring into full play one's own superiority and should adopt a combined operation of naval, air, and ground forces and a tactic of combined guided missile, submarine, and mine assault to enforce a protracted blockade and degrade the opponent's war potential. Second, one should take advantage of the characteristics of large quantity and stealth in submarines and mines to stage offensive mine-laying operations against, and positional ambush near, the main ports and sea lanes of the opponent, to trap its ships in the ports or anchored areas, restrict their movement, and degrade its combat capabilities. Third, one should rely on the broad masses of people and progressive forces in the coastal regions and bring into play their roles in carrying out reconnaissance, mine laying, harassment, and logistic support. [authors' translation]

Blockades are carried out as multistage operations, with the first step being to create a no-fly zone and seize air superiority by, in part, attacking air bases. In addition, outer islands may also need to be seized because they "constitute [enemy] forward positions and form a protective screen for the enemy defense" (Wang and Zhang, 2000, p. 418 [authors' translation]). These operations would then be followed by attacking enemy ports and mining the entrance to harbors. After the port has been neutralized, submarines, followed by surface ships would enter the area of operation and enforce the blockade (Wang and Zhang, 2000, pp. 323–324). The focus of the units enforcing the blockade would be to control waters out to 30 nautical miles from the enemy coast (Wang and Zhang, 2000, p. 415).

Chinese sources on blockade operations emphasize the use of mines and submarines. Mines, to be laid mainly by submarines during the opening stages of a campaign, are considered one of the weapons of choice when carrying out blockade operations (Wang and Zhang, 2000, p. 416). Wang and Zhang (2000, p. 416) observes that mined areas are

> often located near the waters of the main ports in the enemy coastal region and coastal navigation channels. Mine obstacle systems should be made up of several mine zones and widely scattered mines. Every mine zone should be targeted at one important enemy port or navigation channel and should be wide enough and long enough to achieve a certain kill probability and pose a wide threat to the enemy. [authors' translation]

While the use of submarines is stressed in conducting mine warfare, aircraft are also indicated as playing an important role (Wang and Zhang, 2000, p. 416). In addition, 广大人民群众 ["the broad masses of people"], a possible reference to the use of civilian vessels, can be relied on to assist blockade operations, including mine laying (Wang and Zhang, 2000, p. 417 [authors' translation]).

Effectively conducting blockades presents significant challenges. Wang and Zhang (2000, p. 411) notes that, by

> seizing command of the air, sea, and electromagnetic fields as the centerpiece; grasping the key links; striking at the enemy's vital points; and collectively and flexibly employing forces and weapons can one gain a better advantage to accomplish campaign objectives. [authors' translation]

Thus, effectively enforcing a blockade may require the PLA to accomplish many of the requirements of winning a war first.

Enforcing a blockade can be a key element of a prolonged naval campaign. Wang and Zhang (2000, p. 410) stresses that

> unless one is absolutely sure of a victory, one should not rashly engage the opponent for a decisive sea and air battle. One should instead rely on protracted operations, cut off the opponent's sources of high-technology equipment and war materiel supplies, and degrade its war potential. [authors' translation]

One factor complicating the prosecution of blockades is conducting them according to international law. Wang and Zhang (2000, p. 321) recommends that,

> when conducting a sea blockade campaign, we should fully consider the terms of international laws; this is very significant for the political and diplomatic struggle of the nation. On the other hand, it also constrains the work of organization and command to a certain extent and increases the complexity and hardship of accomplishing the task. [authors' translation]

Chinese strategists suggest that PLA forces should conduct unrestricted attacks against enemy military forces but that "official" ships and aircraft should be selectively targeted, and purely civilian vessels that put up no resistance should either be captured or expelled. Third-country vessels should be ordered to leave and those that resist should be boarded (Wang and Zhang, 2000, pp. 412–413). In addition, the time-span and geographic limits of the blockade must be announced before it is conducted, and the geographic limits must not cover third-party territory.

Attacks on Sea Lanes and Ports

Attacks on sea lanes and ports may be conducted independently or in conjunction with blockades and can offer huge rewards. The targets of such operations are "transport ships, shielding forces, ports, intermediate ports, and attack forces with the main targets being transport ships and ports" (Chen, 1991, p. 194 [authors' translation]). One Chinese source (Chen, 1991, p. 191) states that

> attacking freighters and blockading ports are the two most basic measures for destroying sea lines of communications . . . .
>
> Transport ships are the basic means for the enemy to transport materiel, equipment, and troops and are pivotal in changing the potential of a campaign. Destroying or cutting off transport ships can cut off the enemy's front line from the rear and cannot only weaken the enemy's national economy but also its war potential. [authors' translation]

Wang and Zhang (2000, pp. 324–325) also notes that an operation against sea lanes may be protracted:

> This is because, first of all, to protect the safety of sea transportation, the enemy will use different transportation means. Sometimes the enemy will even seize control of part of a sea area, making it impossible for the party that conducts sea transportation sabotage to achieve its campaign goal with one or two attacks. Second, not every sea transportation sabotage campaign will be conducted when we have superiority. When our sea force is in an inferior position, and we want to conduct systematic sabotage against enemy sea transportation lines, the campaign will probably last longer. Third, a sea transportation sabotage campaign usually aims to help combat on the ground battlefield strategically. Thus, it is necessary that the sea transportation sabotage campaign start before the ground campaign that it safeguards and that it end after that ground campaign ends; this makes sea transportation sabotage campaigns last longer. [authors' translation]

One challenge associated with attacking sea lanes is the vastness of the ocean and the scarcity of ships: There are not enough to patrol every avenue of approach. Chinese analysts recommend that the PLA Navy (PLAN) focus its resources on attacking a small number of sea lanes. Such a strategy could be disastrous if the wrong sea lanes were picked. Wang and Zhang (2000, pp. 325–326) states that various targets can be selected for a sea transportation sabotage campaign, and the targets will be scattered over a wide area and be in many places over that area, and combat time is continuous and long. Therefore, according to the goal of a sea transportation sabotage campaign, the importance of enemy transportation lines, and the conditions of the sea area, we should focus on one direction or on one to several enemy transportation lines for sea transportation sabotage combat. Thus, we must deploy our forces judiciously. [authors' translation]

Another source states that this strategy is the only way "the contradiction of 'many lines and few troops' can be resolved and local superiority created to obtain a relatively good effect" (Chen, 1991, p. 190 [authors' translation]).

Chinese analysts also recognize that operations to cut off sea lanes may meet with resistance. One, Chen (1991, p. 190), says that future

campaigns to destroy sea lines of communication will face strong enemy countermeasures. To protect the safety of transport ships, the enemy, in addition to organizing a protective force of ships, will also organize strikes of a certain scale and will attack our campaign forces and the ports and air bases where they are stationed in an attempt to weaken our ability to destroy sea lines of communication and prevent us from effectively conducting strikes or force us to delay this campaign. Under such a situation, our attacking force deployments must not only be focused but must also be in accord with the demands of dispersion to render the enemy's counterattacks unsuccessful. Only in this way can we improve our force's survivability and attack ability. [authors' translation]

A fundamental part of blockading and attacking sea lanes is attacking ports. PLA strategists view ports as vital targets and believe that effectively blockading them can influence the outcome of a war. Chen (1991, p. 203) states that

the important coastal targets of naval bases, ports, and their facilities are central to the stationing, supply, repair, and political work of naval forces and form an important part of the navy's combat ability and war-making potential. Therefore, militarily, politically, and economically, they are very important. The destruction and blockade of enemy bases and ports can weaken an enemy's naval combat ability and war-making potential and crush the enemy's morale. Therefore, this is one of the main responsibilities of the navy and one of the most important campaign types. [authors' translation]

While the strategic value of ports is recognized, they are also known to be heavily defended. To overcome these defenses, Chinese strategists again emphasize the role and value of surprise. Chen (1991, p. 200) states that

> enemy bases often have established tight defenses, and because they are far from our coast, our ability to attack them is limited. Therefore, it is difficult for our forces to achieve overall superiority. Such situations will cause us to employ large-scale attacks and possibly suffer large losses with little result. During the Second World War, the Japanese navy attacked the United States' Pearl Harbor. Because the Japanese achieved campaign surprise, they achieved success with very little cost and almost sank the U.S. Pacific Fleet. The experience from wars proves that achieving surprise reduces losses and achieves a great result. Therefore, it is necessary to comprehensively utilize every measure and work hard to achieve campaign surprise. [authors' translation]

Wang and Zhang (2000, p. 323) states that airpower plays a central role not only in attacking the port but also in preparing the way for follow-on forces and protecting the attacking force from enemy air attack. According to Chen (1991, p. 200),

> when naval air forces attack enemy ports, some of these forces will often suppress and destroy enemy air-defense radars and firepower systems. At the same time, others will be used to conduct assisting attacks against enemy air bases and aircraft carriers that are hindering our main attack force and, thereafter, concentrate attacks against enemy piers, unloading and loading infrastructure, and transport ships. When air forces are attacking the enemy port, some bombers and submarines should be used. In

sea lanes outside of ports, mines are used to hinder and blockade harbors. [authors' translation]

Chinese writings on conducting blockades recognize their importance for waging war. While most discussions of such operations imply that Taiwan is a target, the descriptions are sufficiently general that they could apply to other areas in the western Pacific. In addition, Chinese mention attacking "intermediate" ports, which implies the possibility of striking targets beyond Taiwan.

In trying to conduct blockades, China would face a prolonged operation, long enough to allow U.S. forces time to arrive and conduct counter-blockade operations. While Chinese analysts state that air superiority should be achieved if these operations are to be carried out effectively, the emphasis on submarines and mines in the discussion of blockades suggests that Chinese analysts believe that air superiority may be unachievable or fleeting and that other, more stealthy methods must be employed.[8] Furthermore, Chinese writings do not reconcile the principle of achieving surprise with the need to publicly announce a blockaded area, although it may be assumed that whether a blockade was announced in advance would depend on the specific situation or could follow a surprise attack on military vessels with a subsequent warning to civilian vessels to leave or stay out of the area.

Attacks on Aircraft Carriers

Chinese analysts view aircraft carriers as a key element of the U.S. ability to project power. Considerable effort, therefore, is devoted to identifying ways to neutralize the aircraft carrier threat. The risk to U.S. aircraft carriers such measures present could force the carriers to operate farther from the focus of operations than is ideal, reducing their effectiveness in combat operations against China.

---

[8]   Christensen (2001, p. 31) points out that Peng and Yao (2001) recommends laying mines during periods of bad weather using submarines or combining mine-laying and attacks on surface shipping with information warfare and missile strikes on an enemy's ASW and mine-sweeping assets.

In discussing the need to attack naval targets, such as aircraft carriers, PLA writings are forthright about the challenges of countering a navy with advanced weaponry. Chen (1991, pp. 220–221) states that

> our enemy's medium and large ships often have aircraft or helicopters and medium-range antiship and antiair missiles. The ships have long-range reconnaissance and early warning capabilities, and the area they can control is large. They can conduct long-range offensive and defensive operations. Therefore, these ships ordinarily do not enter their opponent's littorals and especially do not lightly enter into the range of its missiles.
>
> The ocean areas near our country have many islands that can be used, but most of them are nearby and are of limited use for controlling an area. These islands can be conveniently used by our navy, but it will be difficult to surround an enemy force that is conducting long-range operations. For our forces, especially submarines, advancing on the enemy and spending a long time in its operational radius will present serious dangers. [authors' translation]

To overcome these challenges, the PLA may try to wait for opportune times to conduct attacks against naval vessels. Chinese analysts state that naval vessels are particularly vulnerable when a naval group is being redeployed, is undergoing resupply (see fn. 11, p. 74), is passing through a narrow waterway, or when the weather is bad (Chen, 1991, p. 227).

Perhaps the most potent type of naval force is an aircraft carrier strike group. Carrier strike groups not only pose significant problems for the PLAN but would also likely play a major role in U.S. efforts to maintain air superiority over Taiwan and to attack targets on the mainland. According to one Chinese writer, the United States sometimes relies on aircraft carriers for 80 percent of its airpower (Wei Yue-jiang, 2003). Because of this, aircraft carriers are also described as "a great threat to antiair operations in littoral areas and should be resolutely countered" (Cui, 2002, p. 215 [authors' translation]).

Chinese analysts do not believe that aircraft carriers are invincible, however, and have identified weaknesses they think could be exploited (Guo, 2000):

1. Because of its large size, a carrier strike group is difficult to conceal and detectable by radar, infrared, and sonar. In addition, because of its large size, an aircraft carrier is easier to hit than other types of vessels.
2. Air operations from an aircraft carrier can be affected by weather.
3. A carrier strike group consumes an immense amount of supplies.
4. Carrier strike groups have poor antisubmarine and antimine capabilities.
5. The hulls and flight decks of aircraft carriers are susceptible to damage by armor-piercing munitions.
6. While aircraft carriers do carry a large number of aircraft, only a few of them are actually devoted to air defense, around 20. In addition, aircraft launching is sometimes restricted by maneuvers. Thus, it would be possible to overwhelm an aircraft carrier's air defense during certain times.

Several tactics can be used to attack aircraft carriers with ballistic missiles, submarines, antiship missiles, and mines. One source (Wei, 2003) recommends first shooting down an aircraft carrier's early warning aircraft and states that "only by first destroying command, detection, and guidance aircraft can the operational capability of an aircraft carrier be weakened" [authors' translation]. This would also facilitate low-level air attacks that could approach an aircraft carrier from several directions, as recommended by another Chinese writer (Guo, 2000). An article in the popular naval journal 舰船知识 [*Jianchuan Zhishi*] notes that, according to Soviet tactics, submarines would lie in wait for a carrier strike group and ambush it with antiship missiles. The first wave of the strike would use a combination of antiship missiles and antiradiation missiles against ships providing protection to the carrier to weaken the strike group's antimissile capability, but the article also states that going after the carrier in the first wave may be preferable ("The Oscar Class . . . ," 2002).[9]

Chinese strategists appear to base most of their anticarrier tactics on the experiences of other countries (Russia in particular) in contending with carrier forces. Chinese naval strategists seem to have taken special note of an incident involving a Russian Su-27 and an Su-24 that managed to penetrate the defensive airspace of the USS *Kitty Hawk* in 2000. A number of articles in *Liberation Army Daily* consider this episode to be evidence of gaps in carriers' air-defense systems and go into some detail on the methods the Russian aircraft employed (Xu, 2000; Zhou and Xiao, 2000). They place particular emphasis on the effectiveness of the electronic equipment used, such as the "Police Whistle III" radar warning system that supposedly allowed the Russian aircraft to detect and evade U.S. radar and other detection devices.[10]

Another source goes into great detail about a three-stage attack against naval ships using information warfare methods. The first stage is force deployment, in which electronic monitoring by coastal, sea, air, and space-based reconnaissance platforms would locate and collect information on the disposition, location, and direction of movement of an enemy naval force. The PLA would also use deception techniques to misdirect or disperse enemy reconnaissance platforms to make them less able to determine the real objective. This could involve using cover and concealment, as well as fake radio and radar signals. Unmanned aerial vehicles and floating radar reflectors could confuse the air battlespace, while fake submarines and periscopes could flood the sea battlespace. Finally, communications would be strictly controlled so

---

[9] See also, for example, Liu, Zhu, and Hu (1999).

[10] According to the U.S. Navy, the Russian aircraft were detected and tracked from shortly after they took off, 30 to 45 minutes away from the carrier group. The carrier was at a low level of alert, however (consistent with the lack of tensions between the United States and Russia at that time, the Navy stated), and was apparently overflown before any interceptors became airborne. In addition to the low level of alert, the delay in getting aircraft aloft was also partially due to the fact that the *Kitty Hawk* was in the midst of taking on fuel from an underway replenishment ship at the time the Russian aircraft were detected. RAND naval operations specialists state that, in a true emergency, an aircraft carrier would be able to rapidly disengage from the underway replenishment ship and get interceptor aircraft aloft more quickly. (See Jontz and Liewer, 2000, and Dougherty, 2000.)

as not to reveal the true direction or actual forces used (Nie, 1999, p. 185).

The second stage is weakening, in which the PLA would try to tire out and weaken the enemy to create the conditions for a concentrated attack. Unmanned aerial vehicles could harass enemy ships and cause the redeployment of enemy early warning and electronic warfare aircraft and reduce the sortie rate of enemy fighter aircraft. Civilian vessels could place radar reflectors, fake submarines, and fake periscopes into the water to simulate naval platforms, creating "a complex electromagnetic naval battlefield" to cause the enemy to make mistakes (Nie, 1999, p. 185 [authors' translation]).

The final stage is sudden attack. According to Nie (1999, p. 185), hard kills could be used during this phase to

> paralyze the enemy's electronic information systems. We can use the Second Artillery or the Air Force to deliver an EMP bomb to the enemy's large naval force to destroy the enemy's warning and detection systems and operational command systems and other electronic information systems, and can use the air force to attack shipborne radar and early warning aircraft radar with antiradiation missiles to paralyze or partially paralyze the enemy's warning and detection systems and operational command systems. [authors' translation]

Soft-kill methods can be used to jam communication satellites. Nie (1999, pp. 185–186) states that

> jamming satellite communications can block the main channel of information flow. The enemy's naval force and its national military command authorities, naval command centers, and other force links mainly rely on high-frequency satellite communications and microwave communications, and all satellite communications, including commercial and military satellite communications, are easily susceptible to electronic interference and deception. On this point, to attack the transmitters of the high-frequency satellites used by large naval forces, we can use high-powered satellite communication jammers, based either on the ground or on vessels, find an advantageous position within

the satellite's coverage area, then jam the satellite's transmitter at the source, thus ruining its normal operation and interrupting its communication with the outside world. We can also deploy aircraft carrying electronic interference equipment to conduct suppression or deception at the source against shipborne WSC-3 high-frequency communication satellite receivers and SSR-1 satellite signal receivers. [authors' translation]

In addition to these measures, radars will be jammed or destroyed, and Global Positioning System signals will be jammed (Nie, 1999, pp. 186–187).

Information warfare tactics are also emphasized in another text on naval warfare, which advocates attacking the command-and-control functions of a naval group (Chen, 1991, pp. 221–222):

Modern navies are very maneuverable, reflecting high speed and a strong defense. Therefore, their strike needs require a large investment. At the same time, their equipment is highly automated; the technology is complex; and the links between their weapons and equipment are difficult to repair once damaged. Therefore, weaknesses exist. If a strike can be carried out that severely damages a crucial point, it can greatly reduce the operational effectiveness of the target in a short period and may even basically paralyze them, eliminating their combat ability and quickly producing good results. To achieve these results and overcome force insufficiencies, a campaign commander should make paralyzing the enemy's force and destroying the enemy's command capability the main goals early in the campaign. [authors' translation]

This theme was echoed in a January 2003 article concerning attacks on Aegis-equipped destroyers. This article (which was described as the author's own opinion) advocated the use of large numbers (54) of Harpy antiradiation cruise missiles, which would crash into the radars of the destroyers. These attacks would be backed up by antiradiation missiles launched from Su-30 aircraft. After the radars were disabled, additional Su-30s and Kilo-class submarines and Sovremenny destroyers could sink the ships ("Blockade and Kill . . . ," 2003).

Preventing the Use of Bases on Allied Territory

In addition to military antiaccess strategies, Chinese security analysts also discuss a number of diplomatic and political means of denying or limiting U.S. military access to the region in the event of conflict.[11] As noted earlier, Chinese strategists identify reliance on allies for assistance and support, including access to forward bases, as a major vulnerability in U.S. strategy. Although the Chinese writings we reviewed are not always explicit in discussing the end result that China would hope to achieve through 外交方面的斗争 ["diplomatic struggle"], it seems likely that diplomatic and political antiaccess strategies would be at least partly aimed at pressuring countries in the region to deny use of bases and refuse to provide other critical forms of assistance to U.S. forces. At a minimum, Chinese writings reflect awareness that depriving the United States of the ability to use its overseas bases and preventing its forces from receiving other types of support from allies would restrict U.S. military options in the event of a conflict between the United States and China.[12]

According to one military author, for example, local high-technology wars will involve a diplomatic struggle to split the enemy's alliances and isolate the enemy politically and diplomatically to the maximum possible extent. This struggle entails attempts to dismantle an enemy's alliances and improve relations with an enemy's allies. China would do whatever was possible to split or drive a wedge between an enemy and its allies (Jiang, 1997, pp. 133–134). This point is reinforced in Peng and Yao (2001, p. 486), which argues that "split-

---

[11] It should be noted that discussion of political and diplomatic strategies was not nearly as extensive as the discussion of military strategies in the publications we analyzed. This is likely at least in part a result of our choices of publications to analyze, which for the most part were military-operational teaching materials, but it also suggests either that Chinese analysts have not devoted their full attention to assessing the potential utility of diplomatic and political leverage as part of a comprehensive antiaccess strategy or that such discussions are considered more sensitive than discussions of military tactics and operations.

[12] For example, Pan and Sun (1994, p. 237), Li (1995, p. 188), Tang (1999), and Jiang Chuan (1999). The sources we evaluated are usually very general in their descriptions of scenarios, but Peng and Yao (2001, p. 302) contains a brief discussion of dividing alliances as part of a blockade strategy.

ting the enemy's military alliances" [authors' translation] is an important element of a combined military, political, and economic strategy. In another article, published in the journal *China Military Science*, a senior military officer notes that China should exploit potential differences between the dominant member of an alliance and the other members of an alliance. When some alliance members are reluctant to intervene in a conflict, either because they have different views and interests than the dominant ally or because of a weak foundation of domestic political and social support for participation in a conflict, it presents China an opportunity to "break through at weak points . . . warn the other countries, create a chain reaction, and completely undermine the enemy's alliance" (Zhao, 2001). The objectives are to restrict the enemy's freedom of action and to prevent other countries from intervening in the crisis or conflict. To this end, it is also viewed as essential for China to seek greater support from the countries with which it already has strong relationships and to pursue the support of members of the United Nations Security Council, or at least to strive to ensure that they remain neutral (Jiang, 1997, pp. 133–134).

Few of the sources we reviewed refer to specific countries, but Chinese strategists have in interviews clearly identified Japan as the primary target of the diplomatic and political antiaccess strategies. Chinese analysts also assess that, for the United States, the importance of military bases in Japan has increased greatly in the wake of the closure of U.S. bases in the Philippines (Kang Wuchao, 1998). Moreover, they have suggested that diplomatic and political leverage might be sufficient to keep Japan out of a potential Taiwan conflict involving China and the United States. In an interview published in a Chinese academic journal (Zhu, 2001), for example, a professor at China's National Defense University expressed optimism that China would be able to prevent Japan from supporting the United States and intervening in a conflict over Taiwan:

> If the U.S. intervened [in a conflict], we would have to pay close attention to tendencies in Japan. In accordance with the U.S.-Japan alliance and treaty, Japan also will be bound to intervene, but if the time comes, there is reason to doubt that Japan would

act in accordance with the treaty. In my view, Japan would certainly take its own interests as most important, and it is possible that China could make Japan remain neutral. [authors' translation]

In other settings, Chinese military officers have indicated that deterrence and coercion, including threats to use force against Japan, might be required to undermine Japan's willingness to support the United States in a Taiwan scenario. For example, a senior colonel assigned to PLA's National Defense University told a visiting American China specialist that, in the event of a conflict with Taiwan, Beijing would try to coerce Tokyo into refusing to allow U.S. forces to use Japanese bases in the conflict. The PLA officer said that China would "try to deprive the United States [of the] right to use foreign bases—we shall tell Japan that if they allow the United States to use bases there [in the conflict], we shall have to strike them!" (Shambaugh, 2002, p. 309)

As for dealing with the possibility that Washington might look to other countries in the region for support in the event of a conflict over Taiwan, reports in the Hong Kong media suggest that Chinese analysts are generally dismissive of Washington's ability to gain military assistance from other regional actors. Countries like India, Singapore, and Thailand are seen as unlikely to support the United States in a Taiwan conflict scenario. According to one Hong Kong media report, Chinese analysts assess that, "after weighing up the gains and losses in their ties with mainland China and their ties with Taiwan, they would very likely adopt a shirking and passive attitude" (Yi, 2002).[13] This assessment suggests that Chinese analysts calculate Beijing would have to apply relatively minimal pressure on some countries to prevent them from assisting and supporting the United States in any crisis involving Taiwan.

---

[13] As suggested by the title of the article, this observer argues that the prospect of Japanese intervention in a Taiwan Strait crisis is a matter of much greater concern to Chinese military officers and security specialists.

CHAPTER FOUR

Potential Effects of Chinese Antiaccess Measures

If, in a conflict with the United States, China were to employ the measures described in the preceding chapter, they could not only significantly disrupt U.S. military operations as a whole but specifically slow the deployment of U.S. forces to the theater of operations, prevent them from operating from certain locations within the theater, or cause them to operate from distances greater than the U.S. military would otherwise prefer. For analytic purposes, the antiaccess measures described in the preceding chapter can be consolidated into four broad categories: attacks on airfields; attacks on C[4]ISR systems; attacks on logistics, transportation, and support functions; and attacks on aircraft carriers.

Attacks on Airfields

Attacks on airfields in the western Pacific could prevent U.S. aircraft from deploying to them in the first place or compel the aircraft to withdraw to more-distant locations. As noted in the previous chapter, the Chinese concept of operations for attacking air bases entails first damaging runways to prevent takeoffs and landings, then destroying aircraft on the ground. China is said to be developing conventional ballistic missiles that could reach Okinawa and all of South Korea, to have developed submunition warheads for its short-range ballistic missiles, and to have improved their guidance to achieve circular error probable values (CEPs) of less than 50 meters.[1] Therefore, assuming that China possesses a runway-penetrating submunition warhead, it would be possible for China to implement the concept described above against U.S. air bases in Okinawa or South Korea by first using ballistic missiles with runway-penetrating submunitions to shut down flight operations at key U.S. air bases, then by using additional ballistic missiles, as well as aircraft and cruise missiles, to attack the aircraft at these facilities. High-explosive bomblet submunitions delivered by ballistic missiles would be particularly effective in attacking aircraft parked in the open at air bases (Stillion and Orletsky, 1999, pp. 11–15, 23–25). Shelters for protecting large aircraft, such as bombers, AWACS, electronic warfare, aerial-refueling, and transport aircraft have yet to be developed, so these aircraft would be particularly vulnerable to such attacks. Missiles with unitary high-explosive warheads could attack soft targets, such as pilot quarters and ready rooms. Submunitions are generally not capable of penetrating the hardened shelters used to house fighter aircraft at many air bases, however, and even missiles with 50-meter CEPs are not sufficiently accurate to ensure a high percentage of direct hits by unitary warheads. Thus, fighter aircraft in hardened shelters would be relatively safe from Chinese ballistic missile attack. They would, however, be vulnerable to attack by aircraft with precision-guided munitions and land-attack cruise missiles with concrete-penetrating warheads. China is believed already to possess at least some precision-guided air-to-surface missiles and bombs and is expected to field land-attack cruise missiles within the next few years (OSD, 2005, p. 29; Jane's, 2004b).

Chinese aircraft and cruise missiles would normally have difficulty penetrating the fighter screens defending U.S. air fields, but if flight operations had been temporarily suspended because of attacks on runways by ballistic missiles with runway-penetrating submunitions,[2]

---

[1]   This is discussed in the Office of the Secretary of Defense's (OSD's) 2004 *Annual Report on the Military Power of the People's Republic of China*, and by Jane's Information Group [Jane's], 2005b).

[2]   Rapid runway repair capabilities could enable relatively early resumption of flight operations, but the PLA could periodically reattack the runways, extending the amount of time that they were inoperable. However, because each attack would require a significant number

Chinese aircraft and cruise missiles would be able to attack the aircraft and facilities at U.S. air bases in Okinawa or South Korea with relative impunity.[3] China's Su-30 strike aircraft are believed to be equipped with precision-guided munitions and have an unrefueled combat radius of approximately 1,500 km (Jane's, 2004a; Jane's, 2005f),[4] and its H-6 bombers have an unrefueled combat radius of 1,800 km and will soon carry the YJ-63 air-launched cruise missile (Hunter, 2003; Jane's, 2006a).[5] China is developing a ground-launched cruise missile with a range of more than 1,500 km (Jane's, 2004b) and may be developing conventional ballistic missiles with enough range to reach targets throughout Japan (Jane's, 2005a). Thus, it is possible that China will eventually be also able to implement this concept of operations against U.S. air bases in the main islands of Japan.[6]

A final means of attacking airfields consists of using covert operatives (PLA SOF or covert agents under the control of China's non-military intelligence services), who could destroy aircraft or critical facilities, such as control towers and air traffic control radars, or to assassinate key personnel. Figure 4.1 shows the locations of major U.S. air and naval facilities in the western Pacific.

Attacks on C⁴ISR Systems

Attacks on C⁴ISR systems in the western Pacific would not necessarily prevent the deployment of forces to the theater, but could force U.S. forces to withdraw some distance. For example, ballistic missiles, covert operatives, and (if flight operations at nearby U.S. airfields have

---

of missiles to ensure that runways were no longer usable, they could not be kept closed indefinitely.

[3] Except for any SAM systems and any fighters that could be scrambled from nearby unaffected airfields or from aircraft carriers.

[4] China does not currently have an aerial refueling capability for its Su-30s.

[5] China does not currently have an aerial refueling capability for its H-6s.

[6] Other potential operating locations for aircraft, such as the island of Luzon in the Philippines, will be also be vulnerable.

Figure 4.1
Major U.S. Air and Naval Facilities in the Western Pacific

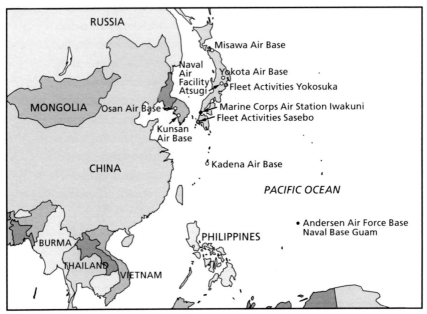

RAND MG524-4.1

been disrupted as described above) cruise missiles and aircraft could destroy command facilities associated with U.S. air forces, significantly degrading local air operations. Given the ranges of China's missiles- and aircraft, command facilities in Okinawa, South Korea, and— eventually—the main islands of Japan would be most vulnerable to such attacks. Cruise missiles, aircraft with precision-guided munitions, or covert operatives could also sever terrestrial communications links and destroy satellite ground stations; high-energy lasers or kinetic-energy antisatellite weapons could blind or destroy U.S. surveillance and reconnaissance satellites[7]; and satellite uplink jammers could interfere with communications satellites. Air- or seaborne jammers could disrupt U.S. land-based or airborne early warning radars;

---

[7]   According to DoD, China is conducting research to develop ground-based laser antisatellite weapons that could eventually be capable of damaging or destroying satellites (OSD, 2005, p. 36).

and long-range SAMs or air-to-air missiles (AAMs) could intercept early warning aircraft.[8] All these actions could degrade the U.S. theater commander's ability to coordinate the operations of forward-deployed forces or the U.S. ability to collect and transmit early warning information, thus increasing the vulnerability of forward-deployed forces to air and missile attacks.

Although the effects of EMP on different kinds of equipment are highly variable, an EMP attack on U.S. military facilities or naval forces in the western Pacific could destroy key sensors, communications systems, or information systems, rendering weapon systems ineffective or command elements unable to command, control, and coordinate forces effectively.[9] If the EMP were produced using a nuclear explosion, moreover, that explosion would also result in ionization of the atmosphere for minutes to hours, disrupting radio communications and the operation of radars in the area of the nuclear fireball (U.S. Air Force, 1998; Headquarters, Departments of the Army, Navy, and Air Force, 1963, Appendix B). A nuclear explosion of sufficiently

---

[8] Historically, this has not been a significant issue because U.S. early warning aircraft were unlikely to have need to operate within range of China's SAMs, and Chinese fighter aircraft were unlikely to be able to approach U.S. early warning aircraft closely enough to attack them. China has, however, recently acquired the Russian S-300PMU1 system, which has a range of 150 km. According to the U.S. Secretary of Defense's annual report on Chinese military power, China will also acquire the S-300PMU2 system, which has a range of 200 km, in 2006 (see Jiang, 2004; OSD, 2006, p. 30). When Russia's S-400 system, which is to have a range of 400 km, completes development, China is expected to acquire it as well (see Jane's, 2005d). China is also said to be developing a SAM designed to home in on the emissions of AWACS and jamming aircraft (see O'Halloran, 2004). Finally, China may be developing or attempting to acquire a 400-km-range AAM based on the Russian Kh-31P (see Hewson, 2004a).

[9] O'Rourke (2005, pp. 60–61) reports that testimony from the 2004 Electromagnetic Pulse Commission asserted that "the assessed consequences of . . . a single-explosion [nuclear EMP] attack, are very somber," "the loss of military capability might be absolutely staggering," and "there's substantial reason to be concerned." The area of nuclear EMP effects is largely determined by the height and location of the explosion. Thus, it would be possible for China to choose the location of a nuclear detonation so that it produced EMP effects over Taiwan and the western Pacific but left mainland China unaffected. According to Glasstone and Dolan (1977, p. 519), for example, a nuclear burst at an altitude of 30 miles would result in EMP effects over a circular area 960 miles in diameter centered beneath the detonation.

high altitude would also result in the excitation of the Van Allen belts; within weeks to months, this would lead to the failure of all satellites in low earth orbit except any military satellites specifically designed to withstand this effect (Mueller and Harris, 2003).

According to OSD (2006, p. 34), Chinese technicians are working to develop short-range radio frequency weapons that could be packaged into missiles (or artillery shells) and launched into the vicinity of radars or command posts, where they would release a radio frequency pulse that would disrupt or destroy electronic systems. Radio frequency weapons might also be deployed on small vehicles or in suitcases, which covert operatives would use to target critical military or civilian infrastructure.

A final type of attack on C⁴ISR systems, computer network attack, could render key computer systems or communications links inoperable, denying weapon platforms vital targeting and early warning information or preventing command elements from being able to command, control, or coordinate forces.[10]

If any of the attacks on C⁴ISR systems described above were sufficiently successful, the effectiveness of forces based or operating in the western Pacific could be degraded to the point that the theater commander would choose to move them farther away, either out of concern for their physical survival or simply as a result of a judgment that, because of the difficulty of commanding and controlling these forces, they would be more effective operating from more-distant locations. Thus, although not directly impeding the ability of U.S. forces to deploy into the theater, attacks on C⁴ISR systems could nonetheless have an antiaccess effect by making these forces to operate from more-distant locations.

Attacks on Logistics, Transportation, and Support Assets

Attacks on logistics, transportation, and support functions could also render U.S. forces unable to operate effectively from forward loca-

---

[10] According to OSD (2006, p. 36), "The PLA has established information warfare units to develop viruses to attack enemy computer systems and networks."

tions. For example, ballistic missiles, cruise missiles, aircraft, or covert operatives could destroy aviation fuel storage and distribution facilities at U.S. air bases in the western Pacific. Given the ranges of China's missiles and strike aircraft, facilities in Okinawa, South Korea, and the main islands of Japan would again be the most vulnerable. Such attacks would limit the amount of time that high-intensity air operations could be sustained from the affected bases. Similarly, destruction of the munitions storage facilities supporting these bases would limit the number of air-to-air or strike missions that aircraft operating from them could perform.

In the case of air bases located on relatively small islands, such as Okinawa, cruise missiles, aircraft with precision-guided munitions, or covert operatives could destroy the limited number of facilities on these islands for offloading fuel or munitions from ships; submarines could mine these facilities or associated harbor entrances; aircraft, surface ships, or submarines could intercept supply ships; and fighter aircraft and long-range SAMs could intercept transport aircraft bringing fuel, munitions, and other supplies to sustain these bases.[11] Once on-hand supplies were exhausted, the aircraft at these bases would no longer be combat effective or would be forced to relocate to other, more-distant, bases.

Aircraft, surface ships, or submarines could also intercept ships transporting equipment for ground forces, and fighter aircraft and long-range SAMs could intercept transport aircraft attempting to convey U.S. ground force troops and equipment (including air-defense or helicopter units) to regions near China (e.g., to Korea, Okinawa, or Taiwan). If ground forces have already been deployed, cruise missiles, aircraft with precision-guided munitions, or covert operatives could destroy fuel, munitions, and other offloading facilities at the ports used to sustain these forces; submarines could mine the facilities and ports; aircraft, surface ships, or submarines could intercept supply ships; and fighter aircraft and long-range SAMs could intercept transport aircraft

---

[11] Attacks on airfields as described above, of course, could prevent transport aircraft from being able to land, at least until China's ballistic missile inventory had been exhausted.

bringing fuel, munitions, and other supplies to sustain these forces, rendering them combat ineffective.[12]

Aircraft, surface ships, or submarines could also intercept underway replenishment ships, limiting the amount of time that conventionally powered naval vessels could remain on station in the combat theater and the number of air-to-air or strike missions that aircraft operating from aircraft carriers could perform. Naval operations would also be degraded if ballistic missiles, aircraft with precision-guided munitions, cruise missiles, or covert operatives were used to destroy facilities at ports for storing, transporting, or loading munitions and aviation and ship fuel onto underway replenishment and combat ships. Again, given the ranges of China's missiles and strike aircraft, U.S. facilities in Okinawa, South Korea, and the main islands of Japan would be most vulnerable to such attacks. Destruction of these facilities would prevent underway replenishment ships from being able to take on supplies or prevent combat ships from receiving supplies by returning to these ports.

China could also use fighter aircraft or long-range SAMs to intercept aerial-refueling aircraft, which would force U.S. combat aircraft to return to base to refuel, limiting the distance from their bases within which they could operate and the amount of time that they could spend in the area of combat operations. Even if aerial-refueling aircraft were not successfully intercepted, the mere threat of interception could force these aircraft to operate farther from Chinese territory, limiting the distances from their bases at which combat aircraft could operate and the amount of time that they could spend in the area of combat operations.[13]

---

[12] In the case of a Chinese invasion of Taiwan, of course, China's ground forces would be vulnerable to the same tactic.

[13] Were China to acquire the S-400 system noted above, for example, U.S. aerial-refueling aircraft would have to orbit at least 400 km from Chinese territory to be safe from SAM attack. U.S. fighters flying combat air patrols over the Taiwan Strait would thus have to fly about 325 km each way from their refueling stations (assuming that their combat air patrols were near the center of the Taiwan Strait, which is about 150 km wide). For an F-15C, which has a maximum combat radius of 1,968 km (Laur and Llanso, 1995, p. 88), this means that nearly 20 percent of its time would be consumed transiting to and from the tanking station.

Ballistic missiles, aircraft, cruise missiles, or covert operatives could also destroy repair and maintenance facilities (or maintenance crew quarters) at air and naval bases in the western Pacific, preventing damaged craft from returning for service and forcing them to relocate to other bases for needed maintenance. The net effect would be a reduction in the number of combat sorties that could be flown from an air base each day or the number of ships that could remain on station near China.

Computer network attack could disrupt the computer systems used to support U.S. transportation and logistics networks. According to OSD (2006, p. 26), "PLA writings suggest a successful computer network attack against these systems could have a disruptive effect on an adversary's ability to generate its forces."

Attacks on Aircraft Carriers

A fourth type of attack discussed in Chinese military writings that could prevent forces from operating within the theater, or at least force them to operate from greater-than-optimal distances,[14] is attacks on aircraft carriers. If a carrier were in port at the beginning of a conflict, a plausible situation given the emphasis on surprise in Chinese doctrinal writings, it would be particularly vulnerable because its location could easily be determined. Then, the carrier might be prevented from leaving port (or damaged while trying to do so) by aircraft and missile attacks, by mines covertly placed at the harbor entrance, or by submarine ambush (using torpedoes or missiles) just after the carrier

---

As a result, about 20 percent fewer aircraft would actually be available for intercept operations at any given time.

[14] The farther from the locus of a conflict an aircraft carrier operates, the less effective it will be, particularly in intercepting enemy air raids on land-based facilities, such as those on Taiwan. When fighters scramble in response to an air raid, the increased transit time will mean that fewer may arrive or that they may arrive too late entirely. When conducting combat air patrols, the increased amount of time spent in transit will mean that fewer aircraft can be maintained on station at any one time. Strike capabilities will also be reduced, although less severely, because longer transit times mean that fewer sorties can be conducted each day.

leaves port.[15] Given the ranges of China's missiles and strike aircraft, an aircraft carrier at port in Japan or South Korea at the beginning of a conflict would be at particular risk from such attacks.

Once an aircraft carrier has left port, finding it would be more difficult. Nonetheless, China already possesses capable maritime surveillance and electronic intelligence aircraft and is developing additional means for locating ships at sea, including over-the-horizon radar, long-range unmanned aerial vehicles, and ocean-surveillance satellites (DoD, 2004, pp. 41, 43–45). These systems, and the ability to integrate and fuse data from multiple systems, would significantly increase China's capability to detect and recognize an aircraft carrier at sea.

Once a carrier had been detected, China would have multiple means of attacking it. One would be with surface ships. China's surface fleet consists of roughly 25 guided-missile destroyers and over 40 guided-missile frigates.[16] The most capable of these are China's Russian-built Sovremenny-class destroyers equipped with the Mach 2+ "Sunburn" ASCM (Hooten, 2004b). The air defenses of all but China's newest destroyers are weak, however, so these ships would be vulnerable to attack from a carrier's strike aircraft, and China's surface ships and their missiles could have difficulty penetrating the carrier's protective screen of escort ships.

A second means of attacking an aircraft carrier would be using land-based aircraft. Each PLAN bomber and fighter-bomber is capable of carrying two to four ASCMs (see Hunter, 2004; Munson, 2003; Jackson, 2003; OSD, 2004, p. 35). If PLAN maintained these aircraft on alert until a U.S. aircraft carrier was detected and surged them to attack a carrier strike group, that strike group could potentially face a

---

[15] Mining a harbor entrance prior to the beginning of hostilities would be highly risky, however. Were China discovered in the act of doing so, it would lose the element of surprise. Moreover, if the harbor mined belonged to a third country, such as Japan, it might cause that country to join the U.S. side when it otherwise would have chosen to stay out of the conflict.

[16] See Jane's (2004c) and OSD (2006, p. 48) for estimates of current numbers of destroyers and frigates in PLAN's inventory.

massed attack from nearly 100 attack aircraft and over 200 ASCMs.[17] Although the carrier's F-18 fighters and Aegis-class escorts have highly capable antiair systems, they could be simply overwhelmed by the sheer number of attackers. Moreover, given that only one U.S. carrier strike group is permanently based in the western Pacific at present and if the U.S. had little or no warning that China was about to launch an attack, only one U.S. aircraft carrier might be present in the first few days of a conflict. A lone aircraft carrier would be particularly vulnerable to such a massed attack. In addition, the supersonic antiship missiles that some of China's naval strike aircraft carry would present significant challenges for U.S. ship defenses (see Hewson, 2004b).

As noted in the previous chapter (p. 76), China has also acquired the Israeli-made Harpy system, a truck-launched antiradiation cruise missile. Once the rough location of an aircraft carrier strike group has been determined, Harpies could then home in on the radar emissions of the aircraft carrier and its escorts. The Harpy has a range of several hundred kilometers, and because it is small and slow, it would be difficult for air-defense radars to detect. Although it would be unlikely to sink an aircraft carrier or major surface ship, it could destroy its radars, rendering it vulnerable to subsequent attack (Jane's, 2004b; Munson, 2004; Ben-David, 2005).

A fourth means of attacking an aircraft carrier at sea would be with submarines. China has more than 50 attack submarines, but most of these are still slow, noisy craft armed only with torpedoes. Given the speed of an aircraft carrier while on station, these submarines, even if they were able to evade detection by the carrier's escorts, would not be capable of intercepting an aircraft carrier. To be attacked, the aircraft carrier would have to venture within torpedo range (8 nautical miles or less) of one of these submarines (Jane's, 2004c; Saunders, 2004c; Saunders, 2004a).

China does, however, have about 20 domestically built submarines equipped with ASCMs, which extend the attack radius of China's submarines to more than 20 nautical miles, and is rapidly building

---

[17] See Jane's (2004c) for estimates of current numbers of H-6s, JH-7s, and Su-30s in PLAN's inventory.

more (Jane's, 2004c; Saunders, 2004a; Saunders, 2004d). Moreover, by 2007, PLAN will have taken delivery of eight Russian-built "Kilo-class" submarines that are equipped with a 120 nm-range supersonic ASCM (Jane's, 2004c; Saunders, 2004e, p. 30; Hooten, 2004a). If these Kilo-class submarines were deployed in the waters around China in a conflict with the United States, any aircraft carriers that China's surveillance systems found would quite likely be within range of at least one of these submarines and thus subject to missile attack, which would significantly challenge U.S. ship defenses. (This missile would likely need multiple hits, however, to put an aircraft carrier out of action.)

China's best chance of sinking or disabling an aircraft carrier, of course, would be not to attack it with a single type of system but, if possible, to attack it with all four types of systems at the same time. Doing so would maximize the number of threats that the carrier strike group would have to contend with at once and thus increase the likelihood that at least some attacks would penetrate the carrier's defenses. China's surface ships and submarines could theoretically attack an aircraft carrier far out on the ocean, but China's Su-30, JH-7, and H-6 naval strike aircraft have unrefueled combat radiuses of 1,500 km, 1,650 km, and 1,800 km, respectively (Jane's, 2005f; Hunter, 2003; Jane's, 2005c).[18] Thus, the greatest risk to U.S. carriers would be when they were less than 1,500 km from China's coast.[19]

Finally, China is apparently attempting to develop the capability to hit a ship at sea with a ballistic missile (OSD, 2006, p. 25). Hitting a moving target, such as an aircraft carrier, with a ballistic missile would require a maneuverable reentry vehicle and probably some type of seeker in the missile warhead. These are daunting technical

---

[18]   China would likely want to escort any air raids on U.S. surface ships with fighter aircraft, of which China's longest-ranged are its Su-27s, which have an unrefueled combat radius of 1,500 km. China does not currently have a capability to aerial refuel any of the above aircraft. (See Jane's, 2005e.)

[19]   The risk would be even greater if a carrier strike group were within range of the Harpy system, which is believed to be at least 400 km (see Munson, 2004).

challenges,[20] but if China succeeded in overcoming them, its ability to threaten aircraft carriers would increase dramatically because such missiles would be extremely difficult to intercept and, given their high speeds, would extensively damage any ship they hit. Some U.S. Navy officials reportedly believe that China may have such a capability by 2015 (Chang, 2005; see also Parsons, 2006; O'Rourke, 2005, p. 63).

---

[20] In particular, the physical effects of the interaction of a hypersonic reentry vehicle with the earth's atmosphere would create problems for any kind of seeker in the reentry vehicle unless measures were taken to slow the reentry vehicle down, which would reduce its lethality.

CHAPTER FIVE

Countering Chinese Antiaccess Threats to U.S. Forces

Although Chinese antiaccess tactics have the potential to disrupt U.S. theater access in the event of a conflict with China, the United States can take a number of measures to counter these threats. These include actions using existing forces and capabilities to reduce the potential effects of Chinese antiaccess measures, as well as acquiring new capabilities or improvements to existing capabilities, for the U.S. military.

Actions to Reduce the Potential Effects of Chinese Antiaccess Measures

To reduce the potential effects of Chinese antiaccess measures, the United States can strengthen passive defenses at air bases, deploy air-defense systems near critical facilities, diversify basing options for U.S. military aircraft, strengthen defenses against covert operative attack, reduce the vulnerability of naval forces to attack while in port, reduce the effects of attacks on C⁴ISR systems, reduce the threat of high-altitude nuclear detonations, and bolster the capabilities of allies.

Strengthen Passive Defenses at Air Bases

Chinese missile and air attacks on U.S. air bases would be critical to a successful antiaccess campaign. Improved passive defenses at key air bases could significantly reduce the effectiveness of such attacks. China's ability to threaten operations from U.S. air bases in the region hinges largely on its ability to use ballistic missiles with runway-penetrating submunitions to damage the runways and prevent aircraft from taking off or landing. Strengthening these runways (e.g., by adding a layer of concrete to them) would decrease the amount of damage each individual submunition would cause, increasing the number of missiles required to render a runway unusable. Assuming some capacity to repair the runway (see next paragraph), this would shorten the amount of time that flight operations would be disrupted before China's supply of ballistic missiles was exhausted. Given that China is apparently developing conventional ballistic missiles designed specifically to reach Okinawa, particular priority should be given to strengthening the runways there.

Similarly, the more rapidly runways can be repaired, the shorter the amount of time they can be kept inoperable. Increasing the runway repair capacity at U.S. air bases in the western Pacific, particularly those on Okinawa, would decrease the time after a ballistic missile attack before flight operations could resume, thus increasing the number of missiles needed to keep an airfield closed for a given period and shortening the time that the airfield could be kept closed.

Hardened aircraft shelters also reduce the effectiveness of missile attacks on air bases. As noted above, high-explosive bomblet submunitions are a significant threat to aircraft parked in the open, but even with CEPs of less than 50 meters, ballistic missiles have a relatively low probability of scoring a direct hit on an aircraft shelter. While submunitions increase the probability of hitting a shelter, they lack the penetrating power to damage the aircraft inside. Thus, ensuring sufficient numbers of hardened shelters to house all the fighter aircraft likely to operate from an air base in a contingency would greatly increase their survivability.[1] Moreover, although the costs and engineering challenges of constructing shelters for large aircraft—bombers, AWACS, electronic warfare, transport, and refueling aircraft—may be prohibitive, shelters capable of protecting at least against damage from submunitions may not be infeasible, and their development is worth investigating.

---

[1]   As noted above, aircraft shelters are potentially vulnerable to attack by aircraft-delivered precision-guided munitions and cruise missiles, but many of the measures described below would significantly reduce the threat from such systems.

Finally, construction of underground fuel tanks, which are much less vulnerable to attack by missiles, aircraft, and covert operatives, would further strengthen passive defenses. The United States should therefore ensure that any air bases in the western Pacific likely to be used in a conflict with China have sufficient underground fuel storage to sustain several weeks of high-intensity air operations.

Deploy Air-Defense Systems Near Critical Facilities

In addition to passive defenses, active air defenses can play a key role in countering Chinese antiaccess threats. First, to the extent to which air-defense systems are capable of intercepting ballistic missiles, they would limit the effectiveness of Chinese ballistic missile attacks. In particular, they could prevent China's ballistic missiles from shutting down runway operations. This in turn would enable U.S. fighters to defend these bases from cruise missile and aircraft attacks. Even if ballistic missile defenses were not able to protect runways completely from attack, they would at least increase the number of missiles China would need to direct at a given airfield to be confident of putting it out of action, which would reduce the number of missiles available to attack other targets and shorten the length of time that flight operations could be prevented.

A second way in which air-defense systems could play a key role in countering Chinese antiaccess threats would be by intercepting cruise missiles and aircraft. Currently, U.S. fighter aircraft would be the best means of intercepting Chinese aircraft and cruise missiles. If ballistic missile attacks on runways prevented aircraft from taking off to defend their base, however, China's aircraft and cruise missiles would be able to attack a range of key targets, including aircraft shelters; command posts; communications facilities; storage, distribution, and loading facilities for fuel and munitions; and repair and maintenance facilities. In this case, surface-based air-defense systems would be crucial in thwarting such attacks.

A number of different types of air-defense systems can contribute to the defense of critical facilities against missiles and aircraft. Currently, the most capable operational land-based air-defense system is the Patriot Advanced Capability-3 (PAC-3) system. When the Terminal

High Altitude Area Defense system becomes available, it will increase capabilities against ballistic missiles, and the Medium Extended Air-Defense System (MEADS) will do the same against low-altitude cruise missiles and aircraft. These systems should be augmented by short-range air-defense systems, such as the Avenger, the Surface-Launched Advanced Medium Range Air-to-Air Missile (SLAMRAAM), or the U.S. Navy's Rolling Airframe Missile. Gun-based quick-reaction systems, such as the U.S. Navy's Close-In Weapon System, could also play a valuable role in defending point targets against cruise missiles that evade other systems.

It is important to note that, if land-based air-defense systems are to contribute to the defense of critical facilities, they must be deployed *before* a crisis occurs. Once hostilities commence, one of the very threats that such systems would be intended to defend against—air and missile attacks on airfields—would likely prevent transport aircraft from delivering them where they are needed. Moreover, the airlift requirements for such systems as the PAC-3 are considerable, meaning that, even if transport aircraft were able to land, a number of days would elapse before a unit could be operational. A conflict between the United States and China could develop very rapidly (especially given the Chinese emphasis on rapid operations noted in Chapter Two); in certain scenarios, such as a Chinese attack on Taiwan, a few days could mean the difference between success and failure.[2]

Sea-based air defenses can also help counter air and missile attacks on critical facilities. An Aegis ship patrolling near Okinawa, for example, would contribute significantly to the defense of that island's facilities from attacks by cruise missiles and aircraft and, to some extent, from attack by ballistic missiles.[3]

---

[2]   After research for this monograph was completed in June 2006, the U.S. and Japanese governments announced a plan to deploy PAC-3 batteries to Kadena Air Base and Kadena Ammunition Storage Area on Okinawa (see Watanabe, 2006; "U.S. to Deploy Intercept Missiles to Japan," 2006).

[3]   By 2009, 18 Aegis ships are to be equipped with the Aegis Ballistic Missile Defense system, although these ships will probably have at most ten interceptors each (see Cortes, 2004; McAvoy, 2005; U.S. Missile Defense Agency, 2006).

It should also be noted that host nations can play a valuable role in countering attacks on critical facilities. The Japanese government has announced its intention to acquire PAC-3 batteries (see Brooke, 2003). These systems are being acquired primarily to counter a possible North Korean ballistic missile attack; however, if deployed near critical U.S. military facilities in Japan, these systems will also be capable of defending the facilities against Chinese air and missile attacks. In addition, Japan has four Aegis destroyers that could be deployed near critical U.S. military facilities; beginning in 2007, Japan plans to equip these ships with a ballistic missile defense capability (Onishi, 2004; "Japan to Buy . . . ," 2006).

Diversify Basing Options for Aircraft

In view of China's potential capability to disrupt operations at U.S. airfields in the western Pacific, particularly those on Okinawa, the United States should be prepared to operate from other airfields in the region in the event of a conflict with China. This would force China to distribute its antiaccess capabilities and resources over a larger set of targets, rendering these capabilities less effective, and would avoid the risks associated with concentrating all assets at a single location. Moreover, given the lack of shelters for large aircraft (such as AWACS, electronic warfare, and aerial refueling aircraft), these platforms should be operated from bases out of range of China's conventional ballistic missiles.

The United States should also consider forward-deploying an additional aircraft carrier in the Pacific. Aircraft carriers departing from the west coast of the United States would need nine to ten days to arrive in waters off of Taiwan, while an aircraft carrier departing from Hawaii could arrive off of Taiwan in about seven days. An aircraft carrier departing from Singapore could, however, arrive in three days, and one departing from Guam could arrive in about two days.[4] Given

---

[4] Assuming an average transit speed of 25 knots. According to O'Rourke (2005, p. 30), although U.S. nuclear-powered aircraft carriers are capable of sustained speeds of more than 30 knots, their average speeds over longer transits might be closer to 25 knots or less because of rough sea conditions and the need for their conventionally powered escorts to slow down for refueling. As they approached Chinese waters, moreover, they would probably be further

the emphasis on surprise or preemption in Chinese military-doctrinal writings, the United States may have little or no warning of a Chinese attack and, given the emphasis on rapid operations in Chinese doctrine, a few days delay in the arrival of U.S. naval forces could have a significant effect on the outcome of a conflict.

Strengthen Defenses Against Covert Operative Attack

As noted above, covert operatives could attack aircraft or key facilities and personnel at airfields; command posts; communications links; fuel and munitions storage, distribution, and loading facilities; key port facilities; and repair and maintenance facilities. Since such attacks would generally originate from host-nation territory outside the U.S. bases, the capabilities of host-nation security forces would be critical to defending against such attacks. The United States should ensure that host nations are prepared to prevent and respond to such attacks and that mechanisms are in place to ensure smooth coordination between U.S. base security forces and host-nation security forces. In addition, U.S. forces should take steps to reduce their vulnerability to the various types of attacks covert operatives might attempt. These steps could include installing antisniper systems, increasing perimeter security, and screening critical areas from outside view.

Reduce Vulnerability of Naval Forces to Attack While in Port

A number of steps can be taken to reduce the vulnerability of naval forces in port, including the aircraft carriers, command ships, logistics ships, and transports that would likely be the focus of Chinese attacks. Preconflict, this would include periodically mapping the sea bottom near harbor mouths using high-frequency sonar. Once a conflict began or became imminent, this would allow rapid detection of any new objects (potential mines) on the harbor bottom. Similarly, hydrophones should be installed near harbor mouths to detect the

---

slowed by the need to avoid ambush by submarines. Sea transit times were calculated using the World Ports Distance Calculator (Distances.com), setting the destination to the northern Taiwanese port of Keelung as a proxy for the waters near Taiwan.

presence of submarines.[5] The United States should also ensure that the U.S. or host-nation navy has assets positioned to respond rapidly to any mining or enemy submarine presence at key ports and facilities.

In addition, in view of the Chinese doctrinal emphasis on surprise and preemption, U.S. naval forces in the western Pacific should immediately go to a state of heightened alert, including activation of air and missile defenses while ships are still in port, whenever there are any indications that China may be preparing to use force against another country, even if that country does not appear to be the United States (e.g., even if China's preparations for the use of force appear to be directed solely at Taiwan). Moreover, given that naval forces are most vulnerable while still in port, ships that are in port when indications of a possible attack are received should put to sea as soon as possible. When they do so, of course, these ships should aggressively patrol for the presence of submarines near the harbor mouth, even if hostilities have not yet begun, because China could be waiting to initiate hostilities by attacking U.S. forces as they leave port.

Reduce the Effects of Attacks on C⁴ISR Systems

Many of the measures described above for strengthening defenses against attacks on critical facilities by missiles, aircraft, or covert operatives will reduce the vulnerability of C⁴ISR systems to physical attack. Given the interest in the topic Chinese military writers have shown, however, it seems likely that, in the event of a conflict with the United States, China will also devote significant resources to computer network attack and related information operations. The effectiveness of such efforts will depend largely on exploiting poor information-security practices. Enforcement of proper security practices for U.S. military information systems can significantly reduce the potential effects of Chinese information operations. Such practices include the elimination of known security vulnerabilities, the use of software encryption, isolation of critical systems from publicly accessible networks, elimina-

---

[5]   The authors are grateful to Rear Admiral (retired) Eric McVadon for suggesting the latter measure.

tion of unencrypted links into secure computers, enhanced user identification measures, and monitoring of network activity.

Given the possibility that China could nonetheless succeed in disrupting U.S. C⁴ISR systems, however, the U.S. military should also maintain (and exercise) the ability to conduct operations without continuous, high-bandwidth communications between units.[6] This could entail using communications technologies that are out of date by modern standards or even completely autonomous operations, without data from remote sensors or direction from higher headquarters.

Reduce the Threat of High-Altitude Nuclear Detonations

Because there is evidence that Chinese leaders may not consider the use of a high-altitude nuclear detonation to represent a violation of China's "no first use" policy,[7] the United States should take steps both to deter and to mitigate the effects of such an act. One such step is to engage Chinese military and political officials on the topic and to communicate that the United States does view this type of action as a nuclear weapon attack (even if it does not directly produce any fatalities) and would therefore consider retaliatory use of nuclear weapons to be a justifiable act of self-defense.

In case U.S. efforts to deter Chinese use of a high-altitude nuclear detonation fail, however, the United States should be prepared to resist and counter the attack. This entails ensuring that all military systems are "hardened" against EMP and identifying, in advance, a set of response options that will prevent subsequent instances.[8]

---

[6]   See Wolthusen (2004) for other reasons the U.S. military should maintain the ability to conduct operations without continuous, high-bandwidth communications between units.

[7]   Personal communication with Michael Glosy, Ph.D. candidate, Massachusetts Institute of Technology, July 2003.

[8]   For a description of how to harden equipment against EMP, see Kopp (1996). Reportedly, the 2004 Electromagnetic Pulse Commission stated that incorporating EMP hardening into the design of a system has historically added about 1 percent to its cost. Hardening systems after they have been designed and manufactured has cost about ten times as much (see Sirak, 2004).

Bolster Allied Capabilities

Regional allies can play a vital role in neutralizing the effectiveness of Chinese antiaccess measures. Even if an ally did not wish to participate directly in the defense of a third country against China, it would want to defend its territory from Chinese incursion. We have already noted the value of allied nations in defending U.S. forces and facilities on their territory against attacks by missiles, aircraft, covert operatives, and mines. Consequently, the United States should help the military and security forces of regional friends and allies ensure that they are prepared to defend their airspaces against Chinese missiles and aircraft, to counter covert operative attacks originating from their territory, and to clear their ports and harbors of mines. Such assistance could take the form of intelligence sharing, training, or provision of key systems and technologies, but most important, it would involve ensuring that regional allies are focused on and have invested in strengthening their capabilities to counter the types of attacks China might employ in a conflict with the United States.[9]

Capabilities to Counter Chinese Antiaccess Threats

The United States can acquire or enhance a number of capabilities that would significantly reduce the potential effects of Chinese antiaccess measures. While the U.S. military already possesses some of these capabilities, we discuss them here because further improvements are desirable. Programs may also already be under way to develop some of these capabilities, but we mention them to highlight the importance of continuing the development program through to acquisition.

---

[9] In September 2005, it was reported that Japan's Ground Self-Defense Forces had developed contingency plans for responding to Chinese attacks, including possible "gurerilla" (i.e., covert forces) attacks, on Japanese Self-Defense Force facilities or on U.S. military bases in Japan in the event of a war between the United States and China over Taiwan (see "GSDF Defense Plan . . . ," 2005). Assuming this report is accurate, it suggests that the Japanese military has begun to take positive steps in this regard.

Improved Ballistic Missile Defenses

Given the antiaccess threat ballistic missiles pose and their potential role in enabling other types of antiaccess threats, a robust capability to intercept and destroy these missiles would be a major contribution to the ability of the United States to counter Chinese antiaccess measures. Existing land-based PAC-3 and sea-based Aegis Ballistic Missile Defense systems provide some missile defense capability, but given the number and variety of conventional ballistic missiles China possesses or is developing, further ballistic missile defense capabilities are desirable. Such capabilities could be provided by land-based, sea-based, airborne, or space-based systems. Given the emphasis on surprise and preemption in Chinese doctrinal writings, land-based systems—if already in place in advance of a crisis—would have the advantage of being able to protect nearby facilities on relatively short notice. Sea-based systems have the advantage of being deployable to where they are most needed, given adequate warning time. Moreover, if China develops the ability to attack ships at sea with ballistic missiles, sea-based ballistic missile defenses will also play a critical self-defense role for carrier strike groups. Given the difficulty of acquiring advance warning of a mobile ballistic missile launch, airborne systems, which are generally designed for boost-phase intercept, would have to be maintained continuously on station near potential ballistic missile launch points to be effective, and the United States would have to have some way of neutralizing the long-range surface-to-air and AAM threat to large aircraft. While space-based ballistic missile defense systems could be useful against conventional ballistic missiles, the defensive systems would have to be able to intercept large numbers of ballistic missiles because the Chinese are fielding so many of them.

Regardless of the specific types of systems involved, the ideal protection for airfields and other critical facilities from large-scale ballistic missile attack would be a layered series of defenses capable of engaging the missiles at multiple points along their flight trajectories. These defenses need not be completely impenetrable to be helpful and effective, but the more layers and the more capable each is, the more effective they will be in reducing the effects of Chinese conventional ballistic missile attacks.

Detecting, Identifying, and Attacking Mobile Time-Sensitive Targets

Although this problem has so far proved extremely challenging, the threat of ballistic missile attack would be further reduced if the U.S. military had the capability to detect, identify, and rapidly attack mobile targets, such as ballistic missile launchers.[10] This capability would also be valuable for countering the antiaccess threat from cruise missiles and long-range mobile air-defense systems.[11]

Advanced Shipborne Cruise-Missile Defenses

China's acquisition of supersonic ASCMs and antiradiation cruise missiles with small radar cross sections means that U.S. Navy ships must be capable of defending themselves against these weapons. Moreover, given that Chinese land-attack cruise missiles targeted against U.S. facilities in the western Pacific would generally have to pass over the ocean, shipborne anti–cruise missile capabilities can contribute to the defense of these facilities against land-attack cruise missiles. This capability would be particularly valuable if land-based air operations were suspended because of ballistic missile attack.

Improved Land-Based Cruise-Missile Defenses

Land-attack cruise missiles could attack a variety of critical targets, including aircraft shelters; command and communication facilities; fuel and munitions storage, distribution, and loading facilities; and repair and maintenance facilities. If China succeeded in suspending air operations through ballistic missile attacks on airfields, land-based air-defense systems would be the primary defense against land-attack cruise missiles. Thus, the capability to intercept low-altitude, small radar-cross-section cruise missiles could be critical to defeating Chinese antiaccess efforts. Existing land-based air-defense systems, such as Patriot and Avenger, can provide some defense against cruise mis-

---

[10] Such a capability would be unlikely to prevent an initial volley of ballistic missiles if that were China's first action in a conflict—the United States would be unlikely to launch a preemptive attack against Chinese territory—but would be extremely valuable in preventing or disrupting subsequent ballistic missile attacks.

[11] For an in-depth discussion of the challenges associated with this problem, as well as possible means of overcoming them, see Vick et al. (2001).

siles, but neither is optimized for this mission. Developmental systems, such as MEADS and SLAMRAAM, which are readily deployable and specifically designed for intercepting cruise missiles, should improve cruise missile defense. In addition, deploying U.S. Navy quick-reaction systems, such as the Rolling Airframe Missile and the Close-In Weapon System, for point defense of critical land-based facilities is worth investigating.

Improved Antisubmarine Warfare Capabilities

China's submarines present a variety of potential antiaccess threats. They could attack aircraft carriers; command ships; or under way replenishment, transport, and supply ships. They could also mine harbor entrances and critical port facilities. Defeating Chinese submarines would therefore be a key element of countering Chinese antiaccess measures. By the U.S. Navy's own admission, however, its ASW capabilities have eroded since the end of the Cold War, although the Navy has recognized this deficiency and is now working to revitalize its capability to perform this mission (see "Another Pacific . . . ," 2003; Jane's, 2003, p. 3). These efforts must be sustained for the indefinite future, and improving the Navy's ASW capabilities needs to remain a priority.[12]

Improved Minesweeping Capabilities

Sea mines could affect the ability of the United States to deploy forces to, or operate within, areas around China in a number of ways. Mines sown before U.S. naval combatants and logistics ships in the region left port could delay or prevent the ships from putting to sea. Mines could also prevent or slow sea deployment of U.S. ground forces or the provision of key supplies, such as fuel, to U.S. bases in the region. Minesweeping is a long-standing weakness of the U.S. Navy, which has traditionally relied on allies to perform this mission.[13] In a conflict

---

[12] See Smith, Sandel, et al. (2005, pp. 4–10) for a description of new ASW capabilities being developed by the U.S. Navy.

[13] According to a report by the Congressional Research Service, "The Navy's mine countermeasures (MCM) capabilities have been an area of concern . . . for a number of years" (O'Rourke, 2005, pp. 34–35).

with China, however, the United States may have relatively little support from allies. Taiwan will likely be preoccupied with keeping its own ports clear. Japan and Korea would undoubtedly provide mine-sweeping assets to clear mines from their own territorial waters but, for both political and time-and-distance reasons, cannot be counted on to clear mines from U.S. facilities outside these nations' territory. The United States therefore needs to have a strong minesweeping capability of its own.[14]

Counters to Antisatellite Attacks

Given the dependence of U.S. military operations on satellite surveillance and communications, counters to potential antisatellite attacks would be vital to defeating Chinese antiaccess threats and sustaining effective military operations more generally. Possible approaches include hardening satellites against antisatellite attack, stealth, building redundancy or the capability to "degrade gracefully" into satellite constellations, acquiring a rapid reconstitution capability, and the ability to retaliate in kind.

Antisatellite Attack

Satellite surveillance and communications could be a critical enabler of many of China's antiaccess measures, particularly efforts to locate and attack an aircraft carrier at sea. Having the capability to disable China's satellites would significantly reduce the potential effectiveness of associated antiaccess attacks. If China also possessed an antisatellite capability, the United States, given its greater dependence on satellites, might not want to be the side to escalate a conflict to space. The United States would nonetheless want a robust antisatellite capability, both to deter China from escalating to space and to be able to respond in kind if China did.

---

[14] See Smith, Sandel, et al. (2005, pp. 11–14) for a description of new minesweeping capabilities the U.S. Navy is developing.

Counters to Long-Range Surface-to-Air and Air-to-Air Missiles

China's possession of long-range SAM systems and potential acquisition of even longer-range surface-to-air and AAMs threaten the ability of a variety of U.S. aircraft to operate near or over China. The potentially affected aircraft include not just fighters but also intelligence, surveillance, and reconnaissance; electronic warfare; transport; aerial refueling; and missile defense aircraft. These aircraft need to be able to operate near or over China with a relatively low risk of interception by long-range active or passive radar-homing missiles. Possible means for providing this capability include stealth, passive surveillance systems, and the ability to defeat antiair missiles, including passive radar-homing missiles.

Highly Capable Long-Range Air Defense

In a conflict between the United States and China, such as one over Taiwan, Chinese antiaccess measures could succeed in preventing U.S. land-based interceptors from using air bases close to China or in preventing U.S. naval forces from operating close to China's shores. Thus, the capability to defend airspaces far from the nearest U.S. air bases or naval platforms would be valuable to countering Chinese antiaccess efforts. One form this capability could take would be extremely long-range sea-based SAM systems, such as the SM-6, which would enable U.S. Navy ships to provide air defense over such areas as the Taiwan Strait while remaining well out to sea.[15] Another form could be fighters capable of defeating several times their number of Chinese counterparts.[16] The U.S. Air Force's F-22 is believed to have such a capability. F-35s, which are the most capable ship-based aircraft that the U.S. Navy and Marine Corps currently plan to acquire, will also have this capability, albeit to a lesser extent.[17]

---

[15] The SM-6 is planned to have a range of 200 nautical miles (370 km) (see Jane's, 2006).

[16] The long transit times for fighter aircraft operating from distant land bases or aircraft carriers would mean both that only aircraft already on combat air patrol at the time of a Chinese air raid would able be to respond to it and that the number that could be maintained on combat air patrol at any one time would be limited.

[17] For a description of the capabilities of the F-35, see Verschaeve (2006).

Early Strategic and Tactical Warning

As noted in multiple places above, Chinese antiaccess measures would be significantly more effective if China achieved strategic and/or tactical surprise in launching preemptive attacks on U.S. forces. Improved strategic and tactical warning of a Chinese attack would therefore significantly enhance the ability of the United States to counter Chinese antiaccess measures. In view of China's current and known developmental military capabilities, U.S. air and naval forces in Okinawa, South Korea, and the main islands of Japan would be at greatest risk from such an attack. Even ambiguous warning would allow the United States to put naval assets to sea, activate missile defenses, and deploy or disperse air assets, all of which would substantially reduce the effects of Chinese antiaccess measures.

CHAPTER SIX

Conclusion

The possibility of a Chinese antiaccess strategy is more than hypothetical. Although the Chinese military doctrinal writings we reviewed for this study do not reflect an explicit antiaccess concept, they do discuss a wide range of tactics that could slow the deployment of U.S. forces to the theater of operations, prevent them from operating from certain locations within the theater of operations, and/or cause them to operate from distances greater than the U.S. military would otherwise prefer. For example, a combination of ballistic missile, cruise missile, aircraft, and covert operative attacks on runways, aircraft, shelters, and other critical facilities could render U.S. airfields in Okinawa, South Korea, and the main islands of Japan unusable, particularly in the early days of a conflict. In addition, ballistic missile, cruise missile, aircraft, covert operative, jammer, antisatellite, EMP, and computer network attacks could degrade command-and-control or early warning capabilities for forward-deployed forces, particularly air forces operating from bases within about 1,500 km of China, to the point that the theater commander would choose to move them farther away.

Similarly, ballistic missile, cruise missile, aircraft, covert operative, naval, submarine, mine, and long-range SAM attacks—on storage, transportation, and loading facilities for fuel or munitions; on transport aircraft or ships for troops, fuel, or munitions; or on repair and maintenance facilities—could prevent the deployment or sustainment of forces at forward locations, such as Taiwan or Korea. Attacks by aircraft, surface ships, submarines, mines, antiradiation drones, and perhaps even ballistic missiles could force aircraft carriers to operate more than 1,500 km from China's coast or risk being disabled or sunk (thus denying naval aviation a platform from which to operate). Figure 6.1 shows the portions of the western Pacific that are most vulnerable to Chinese antiaccess measures.

As a consequence of all this, it is possible that the United States could actually be defeated in a conflict with China—not in the sense that the U.S. military would be destroyed but in the sense that China would accomplish its military-political objectives while preventing the United States from accomplishing some or all of its own political and military objectives. A weakened initial U.S. response to a Chinese assault on Taiwan, for example, could result in the collapse of Taiwan's military resistance. The island might therefore capitulate before the United States could bring all its combat power to bear. If that were to

Figure 6.1
"The Dragon's Lair"—Portions of the Western Pacific Most Vulnerable to Chinese Antiaccess Measures

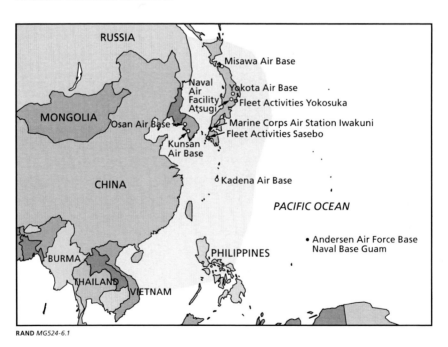

RAND MG524-6.1

happen, it seems unlikely that the United States would continue the conflict, even though U.S. military power would largely be intact.

A Taiwan scenario may be unusual in the extremely high premium associated with a rapid U.S. response, but it is not the only conceivable scenario in which a delayed or degraded initial U.S. response could make it significantly more difficult for the United States to reverse the results of China's actions. A combined Chinese–North Korean invasion of South Korea, for example, if it succeeded in occupying the entire Korean peninsula, would also be extremely difficult for the United States to reverse. Although it presumably would take China weeks rather than days to occupy the entire Korean peninsula, U.S. ground forces would play a more-important role in resisting such an invasion than they would in an invasion of Taiwan, and the deployment timelines for significant amounts of ground forces would also be measured in weeks and months. Thus, Chinese antiaccess measures in the initial stages of a conflict on the Korean peninsula could still have a significant influence on the outcome.

Even if Chinese antiaccess measures did not result in the outright defeat of the United States, they would likely make it significantly more costly for the United States to operate in the region. Moreover, it is possible that these costs could rise enough that, even if U.S. decisionmakers were confident that the United States would eventually prevail in a conflict with China, they might be unwilling to pay those costs.

Finally, even if the tactics described above did not result in the United States being unwilling or unable to defeat China, it is possible that Chinese decisionmakers could convince themselves that they *would* cause the United States to be unwilling or unable to intervene successfully. China could consequently take actions that would bring it into conflict with the United States. That is, Chinese belief in the effectiveness of antiaccess and other asymmetric strategies could result in the failure of U.S. deterrence and a costly and bloody conflict that otherwise would not have occurred.

The United States can, however, take a number of actions to counter Chinese antiaccess threats. Strengthening passive defenses at air bases, deploying air and missile defense systems, strengthening defenses against covert operatives, and bolstering allied air-defense capabilities will reduce the vulnerability of air bases to antiaccess attacks. Diversifying basing options for aircraft will diminish the effects of such attacks even if they are successful. Air and missile defense systems, strengthened defenses against covert operatives, improved allied defensive capabilities, improved information-security practices, and efforts both to deter and to mitigate the potential effects of high-altitude nuclear detonations can reduce the vulnerability of C⁴ISR and logistics systems to antiaccess attacks. Maintaining the ability to conduct operations without continuous high-bandwidth communications between units will diminish the effects of attacks on C⁴ISR systems even if they are successful. Preconflict mapping of the sea bottom and installation of hydrophones near harbor mouths, as well as strategic positioning of mine-clearing and antisubmarine assets, will reduce the vulnerability of ships in port, as will putting naval combatants on a heightened state of alert and sending them to sea as soon as possible whenever there are any indications that China may be preparing to use force in the region. Moreover, because of the concern that Chinese decisionmakers could convince themselves that antiaccess tactics might cause the United States to be unwilling or unable to intervene successfully in a conflict, the actions described above should be openly publicized so as to reduce the likelihood that China might be willing to risk a confrontation with the United States.[1]

In addition, the United States can acquire or improve a number of capabilities to further enhance its ability to counter Chinese antiaccess strategies. Improved ballistic missile defenses and a capability to detect, identify, and attack mobile, time-sensitive targets would reduce the ballistic missile threat to air bases; to C⁴ISR and logistic facilities; and, if China acquires the capability, to ships at sea. Improved land-based and advanced shipborne cruise missile defenses would reduce the cruise missile threat to air bases, C⁴ISR and logistics facilities, and ships at sea. Improved ASW and minesweeping capabilities would reduce the submarine and mining threats to key surface ships and ports. Counters to antisatellite attack and the United States' own antisatellite capability would respectively reduce the threat to U.S. satellites and to ships

---

[1] So long as doing so would not compromise the effectiveness of these actions.

at sea, particularly aircraft carriers. A highly capable long-distance air-defense ability and counters to long-range SAMs and AAMs would reduce the threat to U.S. intelligence, surveillance, and reconnaissance aircraft and enable the U.S. military to defend airspaces near China even if Chinese antiaccess tactics against airfields and aircraft carriers were successful. Finally, early strategic and tactical warning capabilities would substantially reduce the potential effects of a wide range of Chinese antiaccess measures.

The Chinese military writings we have examined do not address in any detail the strategic trade-offs Chinese decisionmakers would be forced to confront in weighing whether or not to order the PLA to employ certain antiaccess approaches in a conflict with the United States.[2] At the strategic level, Beijing would likely seek to prevent the scope of conflict from expanding and avoid causing third parties to become directly involved in a conflict between the United States and China (although such countries might nonetheless allow U.S. forces to operate out of bases on their territory). Although some of the antiaccess approaches discussed in this study would be highly valuable to China at the operational level, they would seriously undermine the chances of achieving the higher-level political objectives. Employment of antiaccess measures would risk sparking horizontal and vertical escalation, potentially broadening the geographic scope and increasing the intensity and destructiveness of the conflict. Attacks on U.S. bases in Japan or Korea, for example, would greatly increase the likelihood that Tokyo or Seoul would participate more actively in a conflict, and any attacks against bases on U.S. territory, such as Guam or Hawaii (China's current capability to attack bases in Guam or Hawaii is extremely limited, but could increase in the future), or perhaps against such high-value platforms as aircraft carriers or space assets, would risk sparking the escalation of what might otherwise be a limited conflict. Nonetheless, we judge that Beijing may well be willing to run some of these risks in a conflict over Taiwan, especially if senior leaders perceived that

---

[2]   Inferring national intentions and leadership preferences from operational-level military writings would likely result in major analytical errors. We have thus attempted to avoid doing so in this study.

the survival of the current regime was at stake. Moreover, because of the Chinese emphasis on striking early in a conflict, the United States must also be prepared for the possibility that it may not have deployed needed forces to the theater before combat starts. Indeed, any move to deploy forces to the theater, even one intended to deter rather than initiate conflict, could trigger a preemptive Chinese attack on U.S. forces.

There is much the United States can do to mitigate the antiaccess threat. Some of the measures required cost relatively little, such as deploying existing air-defense systems and mine-clearing assets to locations near critical facilities in the western Pacific, preparing to operate from alternative airfields in the region, ensuring that mechanisms are in place to ensure smooth coordination between U.S. base security forces and host-nation security forces in responding to covert operative attacks on U.S. bases, preconflict mapping of harbor bottoms, enforcing proper information-system security practices, and maintaining and exercising the capability to conduct combat operations without continuous, high-bandwidth communications between units. Others, however, will require substantial resources, and still others may require fundamental reassessment of operational doctrine and plans. Failure to respond to the Chinese antiaccess threat, however, will put potential U.S. military operations against China at increasing risk, particularly as China's military capabilities increase in the future. The Chinese antiaccess threat is real and growing, but it can be overcome if the U.S. military devotes the necessary thought and resources to defeating it.

Bibliography

"The Access Issue," *Air Force Magazine,* Vol. 81, No. 10, October 1998.

Albert, Garret, Michael Chase, Kevin Pollpeter, and Eric Valko, "China's Preliminary Assessment of Operation Iraqi Freedom," *Chinese Military Update,* Vol. 1, No. 2, July 2003.

"Another Pacific Carrier Possible," *Washington Times,* October 2, 2003, p. 7.

Barber, Arthur H., and Delwyn L. Gilmore, "Maritime Access: Do Defenders Hold All the Cards?" *Defense Horizons,* October 4, 2001.

Ben-David, Alon, "US Pressure Threatens Israel-China Trade," *Jane's Defence Weekly,* January 12, 2005.

Blaker, James R., *United States Overseas Basing: An Anatomy of the Dilemma,* New York: Praeger, 1990.

"Blockade and Kill Taiwan Independence's 'Aegis,'" *Xiandai Bingqi,* January 2, 2003, pp. 41–44. In Foreign Broadcast Information Service as "PRC: Joint Tactics for Destroying 'Aegis,' 'Arleigh Burke' Described," April 9, 2003.

Bowie, Christopher J., *The Anti-Access Threat and Theater Air Bases,* Washington, D.C.: Center for Strategic and Budgetary Assessments, 2002.

Brooke, James, "Japan Seeks Shield for North Korean Missiles," *New York Times,* August 30, 2003.

Bucchi, Mike, and Mike Mullen, "Sea Shield: Projecting Global Defensive Assurance," *U.S. Naval Institute Proceedings*, Vol. 128, No. 11, November 2002.

Chang, Yihong, "Is China Building a Carrier?" *Jane's Defence Weekly,* August 17, 2005.

陈访友 [Chen Fangyou], 《海军战役学教程》 [*Naval Campaign Teaching Materials*], Beijing: 国防大学出版社 [National Defense University Press], 1991.

Chen Huan, "The Third Military Revolution," in Pillsbury (1998), pp. 389–398.

Christensen, Thomas J., "Posing Problems Without Catching Up: China's Rise and the Challenge to U.S. Security Policy," *International Security*, Vol. 25, No. 4, Spring 2001, pp. 5–40.

Cohen, William, *Report of the Quadrennial Defense Review*, Washington D.C.: U.S. Department of Defense, May 1997.

Correll, John T., "Fighting Under Attack," *Air Force Magazine*, Vol. 71, No. 10, October 1988.

Cortes, Lorenzo, "Surface Warfare Chief Identifies Primary Anti-Access Threats," *Defense Daily*, July 9, 2004.

Coté, Owen R., *Assuring Access and Projecting Power: The Navy in the New Security Environment*, Cambridge, Mass.: MIT Security Studies Program, 2001.

Cruz de Castro, Renato, "The Revitalized Philippine-U.S. Security Relations: A Ghost from the Cold War or an Alliance for the 21st Century?" *Asian Survey*, Vol. 43, No. 6, November–December 2003, pp. 971–988.

崔长崎 [Cui Changqi], 《二十一世纪空袭与反空袭》 [*21st Century Air Attacks and Counter Air Attacks*], Beijing: 解放军出版社 [Liberation Army Press], 2002.

戴清民 [Dai Qingmin], 《信息作战概论》 [*Introduction to Information Operations*], Beijing: 解放军出版社 [Liberation Army Press], 1999.

Dai Qingmin, "On Integrating Network Warfare and Electronic Warfare," *Zhongguo Junshi Kexue,* February 1, 2002. In Foreign Broadcast Information Service as "Chinese Military's Senior EW Official Explains China's Network Warfare Doctrine," June 24, 2002.

Davis, Paul K., Jimmie McEver, and Barry Wilson, *Measuring Interdiction Capabilities in the Presence of Anti-Access Strategies: Exploratory Analysis to Inform Adaptive Strategy for the Persian Gulf*, Santa Monica, Calif.: RAND Corporation, MR-1471-AF, 2002. As of February 5, 2006:
http://www.rand.org/pubs/monograph_reports/MR1471/

Defense Science Board, *Report of the Defense Science Board Task Force on Strategic Mobility*, Washington, D.C., August 1996.

Ding Henggao, "New Defense Science and Technology Strategy to Emphasize Technology Transfer to Civilian Use," *Zhongguo Junshi Kexue*, No. 3, August 20, 1995. In Foreign Broadcast Information Service as "COSTIND Director Ding Henggao on Defense S&T," August 20, 1995.

Distances.com, "World Ports Distances Calculator," Web page, 2006. As of July 6, 2006:
http://www.distances.com

DoD—*See* U.S. Department of Defense.

董德元 [Dong Deyuan], 高善贵 [Gao Shangui], 卢兴波 [Lu Xingbo], and 漆明贵 [Qi Minggui], 〈电子战与活力战有机结合, 增强联合作战的综合打击效能〉 ["Organically Combine Electronic Warfare and Firepower Warfare to Strengthen the Comprehensive Strike Capability of Joint Operations"], in Military Studies Editorial Department (1999).

Dougherty, Jon E., "Russian Flyover Takes Navy by Surprise?" *WorldNetDaily. com*, December 7, 2000.

DSB—*See* Defense Science Board.

Du Fuzheng, "An Analysis of the 'Zero Death Toll' Phenomenon," *Jiefangjun Bao*, May 9, 2000. In Foreign Broadcast Information Service as "Jiefangjun Bao on 'Zero Death Toll' in NATO Raid on Kosovo," May 9, 2000.

Finkelstein, David M., "China's National Security Strategy," in Mulvenon and Yang (1999) pp. 99–145.

———, "Thinking About the PLA's 'Revolution in Doctrinal Affairs,'" in Mulvenon and Finkelstein (2005), pp. 1–27.

Fravel, M. Taylor, "Online and On China: Research Sources in the Information Age," *China Quarterly*, No. 163, September 2000, pp. 821–842.

———, "The Revolution in Research Affairs: Online Sources and the Study of the PLA," in Mulvenon and Yang (2003), pp. 821–842.

Fredericksen, Donald N., Michael B. Donley, and John R. Backschies, "Global Reconnaissance-Strike: Innovative Concept Leverages Existing Program for Early Answer to Anti-Access Challenge," *Armed Forces Journal International*, Vol. 137, No. 11, June 2000.

Friedman, Norman, "Globalization of Anti-Access Strategies?" in Sam J. Tangredi, ed., *Globalization and Maritime Power*, Washington, D.C.: National Defense University, 2002.

Glasstone, Samuel, and Philip J. Dolan, eds., *The Effects of Nuclear Weapons*, 3rd ed., Washington, D.C.: U.S. Department of Energy, 1977.

Godwin, Paul, "Chinese Military Strategy Revised: Local and Limited War," *The Annals of the American Academy*, January 1992.

———, "Compensating for Deficiencies: Doctrinal Evolution in the Chinese People's Liberation Army: 1978–1999," in Mulvenon and Yang (2001).

———, "The PLA Faces the Twenty-First Century: Reflections on Technology, Doctrine, Strategy, and Operations," in Lilley and Shambaugh (1999).

Goldstein, Lyle, and William Murray, "Undersea Dragons: China's Maturing Submarine Force," *International Security*, Vol. 28, No. 4, Spring 2004, pp. 161–196.

"GSDF Defense Plan Prepares for Attacks from China," *Asahi Shimbun*, September 27, 2005.

Guo Xilin, "The Aircraft Carrier Formation Is Not an Unbreakable Barrier," *Guangming Ribao*, December 26, 2000. In Foreign Broadcast Information Service as "PRC Article Describes Shortcomings of Aircraft Carrier Formations," December 29, 2000.

Halliday, John M., *Tactical Dispersal of Fighter Aircraft: Risk, Uncertainty, and Policy Recommendations*, Santa Monica, Calif.: RAND Corporation, N-2443-AF, 1987. As of February 5, 2007:
http://www.rand.org/pubs/notes/N2443/

Headquarters, Departments of the Army, Navy, and Air Force, *Staff Officers Field Manual: Nuclear Weapon Employment Effects Data,* Washington, D.C., FM 101-31-3, Change 1, 1963.

Headquarters U.S. Air Force, Future Concepts and Transformation Division, *The U.S. Air Force Transformation Flight Plan*, 2004. As of February 13, 2006:
https://www.xp.hq.af.mil/xpx/docs/
AFTransFlightPlan2003FinalPubliclyReleasableVersion.pdf

Hewson, Robert, "YJ-91, KR-1 (Kh-31P)," *Jane's Air-Launched Weapons,* May 20, 2004a.

———, "AS-17 'Krypton' (Kh-31A, Kh-31P), YJ-9/KR-1," *Jane's Air-Launched Weapons*, September 6, 2004b.

Hooten, E. R., "SS-N-21 'Sampson' (P-1000 3M70 Vulkan/3M10/3M54 Granat)/ SS-N-27 'Sizzler' (3M51 Biryuza/Alfa)," *Jane's Naval Weapon Systems*, July 12, 2004a.

———, "SS-N-22 'Sunburn' (3M80/3M82 Moskit)," *Jane's Naval Weapon Systems,* August 27, 2004b.

Huang Jialun, "Attach Importance to Operation at Outer Strategic Line," *Jiefangjun Bao*, November 30, 1999, p. 6. In Foreign Broadcast Information Service as "Operation at the Outer Strategic Line Viewed," December 14, 1999.

Huang Xing and Zuo Quandian, "Holding the Initiative in Our Hands in Conducting Operations, Giving Full Play to Our Own Advantages to Defeat Our Enemy: A Study of the Core Idea of the Operational Doctrine of the People's Liberation Army," *Zhongguo Junshi Kexue*, No. 4, November 20, 1996, pp. 49–56. In Foreign Broadcast Information Service as "Operational Doctrine for High-Tech Conditions," June 17, 1997.

Hunter, Jamie, "Xian H-6," *Jane's Aircraft Upgrades*, May 23, 2003.

———, "TUPOLEV Tu-16," *Jane's All the World's Aircraft,* February 10, 2004.

International Institute for Strategic Studies, *The Military Balance 1990–1991,* London: Brassey's, 1990.

Jackson, Paul, "SUKHOI Su-30M," *Jane's All the World's Aircraft*, October 16, 2003.

Jane's—*See* Jane's Information Group.

Jane's Information Group, "US Navy Works to Re-Invigorate Anti-Submarine Warfare in the Littorals," *Jane's International Defence Review*, October 2003.

———, "China Accepts Su-30MK2 Fighters," *Jane's Defence Weekly*, March 31, 2004a.

———, "China Tests New Land-Attack Cruise Missile," *Jane's Missiles and Rockets*, October 1, 2004b.

———, "Navy, China," *Jane's Sentinel Security Assessment—China and Northeast Asia*, May 27, 2004c.

———, "CSS-5 (DF-21)," *Jane's Strategic Weapon Systems*, June 8, 2005a.

———, "CSS-6 (DF-15/M-9)," *Jane's Strategic Weapon Systems*, June 8, 2005b.

———, "XAC JH-7," *Jane's All the World's Aircraft*, October 3, 2005c. As of February 10, 2006: http://online.janes.com).

———, "Almaz/Antei S-400 Triumf (Triumph) (SA-20) Low-to-High-Altitude Surface-to-Air Missile System," *Jane's Land-Based Air Defense*, November 18, 2005d.

———, "Sukhoi Su-27," *Jane's All the World's Aircraft*, December 19, 2005e.

———, "Sukhoi Su-30M," *Jane's All the World's Aircraft*, December 19, 2005f.

———, "KD-63," *Jane's Air-Launched Weapons*, January 18, 2006a.

———, "RIM-66/67/156/161 Standard Missile 1/2/3/5/6," *Jane's Naval Weapon Systems*, February 24, 2006b.

"Japan to Buy 36 Missiles by 2010," *Japan Times*, January 11, 2006.

Jiang Chuan, "Using 'Operation Allied Force' to Explain the 'Unbalanced Operations' of U.S. Forces," *Liaowang*, April 12, 1999. In Foreign Broadcast Information Service as "Operation Allied Force Analyzed," April 21, 1999.

Jiang, Jintao, "Russia Delivers Air Defense Systems to China," *Jane's Defence Weekly*, August 18, 2004.

蒋磊 [Jiang Lei], 《现代以劣胜优战略》 [*Modern Strategy for Using the Inferior to Defeat the Superior*], Beijing: 国防大学出版社 [National Defense University Press], 1997.

Jiao Wu and Xiao Hui, "Modern Limited War Calls for Reform of Traditional Military Principles," *Guofang Daxue Xuebao*, No. 11, November 1, 1987. In Joint Publication Research Service, *China Report No. 037*, July 12, 1988, p. 49, quoted in Godwin (1992), p. 194.

Jontz, Sandra, and Steve Liewer, "U.S. Kitty Hawk Has Changed Response-Time Procedures," *Stars and Stripes*, December 9, 2000.

Kang Wuchao, "Will US Troops Be Withdrawn from Their Okinawa Bases?" *Shijie Zhishi*, December 1, 1998. In Foreign Broadcast Information Service as "Article on US Withdrawal from Okinawa," December 1, 1998.

Kopp, Carlo, "The Electromagnetic Bomb—A Weapon of Electrical Mass Destruction," *Aerospace Power Chronicles*, 1996. As of January 25, 2006: http://www.globalsecurity.org/military/library/report/1996/apjemp.htm

Krepinevich, Andrew F., Jr., *The Military-Technical Revolution: A Preliminary Assessment*, Washington, D.C.: Center for Strategic and Budgetary Assessments, 2002. As of December 22, 2004: http://www.csbaonline.org/4Publications/Archive/R.20021002.MTR/ R.20021002.MTR.pdf

Krepinevich, Andrew, Barry Watts, and Robert Work, *Meeting the Anti-Access and Area-Denial Challenge*, Washington, D.C.: Center for Strategic and Budgetary Assessments, 2003. As of December 22, 2004: http://www.csbaonline.org/4Publications/Archive/R.20030520.Meeting_the_ Anti-A/R.20030520.Meeting_the_Anti-A.pdf

Larson, Eric, Derek Eaton, Paul Elrick, Theodore Karasik, Robert Klein, Sherrill Lingel, Brian Nichiporuk, Roby Uy, and John Zavadil, *Assuring Access in Key Strategic Regions: Toward a Long-Term Strategy*, Santa Monica, Calif.: RAND Corporation, MG-112-A, 2003. As of February 5, 2007: http://www.rand.org/pubs/monographs/MG112/

Laur, Timothy M., and Steven L. Llanso, *Encyclopedia of Modern U.S. Military Weapons*, New York: Berkley Books, 1995.

Li Bingyan, "Recognizing One's Own Historical Place in the Flood Tide of Reform: Written on the Conclusion of Discussion of the Topic 'Is Warfare Gradually Softening?'" *Jiefangjun Bao*, December 26, 2000. In Foreign Broadcast Information Service as "Jiefangjun Bao Discusses PRC Military Change," December 26, 2000.

Li Hechun and Chen Yourong, "Sky War—A New Form of War That Might Erupt in the Future," *Liberation Army Daily*, January 17, 2001, p. 17. In Foreign Broadcast Information Service as "PLA Article Says Space War May Be Future Form of Warfare," January 17, 2001.

Li, Nan, "The PLA's Evolving Campaign Doctrine and Strategies," in Mulvenon and Yang (1999), pp. 146–174.

李庆山 [Li Qingshan], 《新军事革命与高技术战争》 [*The RMA and High-Technology War*], Beijing: 军事科学出版社 [Military Science Press], 1995.

Li Xinliang, "Hi-Tech Local Wars' Basic Requirements for Army Building," *Zhongguo Junshi Kexue*, November 20, 1998. In Foreign Broadcast Information Service as "Li Xinliang on High-Tech Local War," May 17, 1999.

Lilley, James R., and David Shambaugh, eds., *China's Military Faces the Future*, New York: M.E. Sharpe, 1999.

Liu Jiangping, Zhu Weitao, and Hu Zili, "A Move Essential for Disintegrating the Enemy's Combined Aerial Attacks—If the Federal Republic of Yugoslavia Attacked NATO's Aircraft Carrier-Led Battle Groups in the Adriatic Sea," *Liberation Army Daily*, August 17, 1999, p. 6. In Foreign Broadcast Information Service as "Jiefangjun Bao Article on FRY Defense," August 17, 1999.

Liu Lisheng, "Okinawan Public's Anti-US Bases Activities Increasing," *Zhongguo Xinwen She*, undated. In Foreign Broadcast Information Service as "ZXS 'Newsletter' on 'Increasing' Okinawan Public's Anti-US Bases Activities," July 23, 2000.

鲁道海 [Lu Daohai], 《信息作战:夺取制信息权的探索》 [*Information Operations: Exploring the Seizure of Information Control*], Beijing: 军事谊文出版社 [Junshi Yiwen Press], 1999.

Lu Linzhi, "Preemptive Strikes Crucial in Limited High-Tech Wars," *Jiefangjun Bao*, February 14, 1996, p. 6. In Foreign Broadcast Information Service as "Preemptive Strikes Endorsed for Limited High-Tech War," February 14, 1996.

McAvoy, Audrey, "Pacific Rim on Cutting Edge of Ballistic Missile Defense," *Honolulu Advertiser*, December 26, 2005.

McKenzie, Kenneth F., *The Revenge of the Melians: Asymmetric Threats and the Next QDR*, Washington, D.C.: Institute for Strategic Studies, McNair Paper 62, 2000.

Medeiros, Evan S., "Undressing the Dragon: Researching the PLA Through Open Source Exploitation," in Mulvenon and Yang (2003), pp.119–168.

Metz, Steven, and Douglas V. Johnson II, *Asymmetry and U.S. Military Strategy: Definition, Background, and Strategic Concepts*, Carlisle Barracks, Pa.: Strategic Studies Institute, 2001.

军事学术编辑部 [Military Studies Editorial Department], 《我军信息战问题研究》 [*Research on Our Army's Information Warfare Issue*], Beijing: 国防大学出版社 [National Defense University Press], 1999.

Mueller, Karl P., and Elwyn D. Harris, "Anti-Satellite Attack," *The Atlantic Monthly*, July–August 2003, p. 87.

Mulvenon, James, "The PLA and Information Warfare," in Mulvenon and Yang (1999), pp.175–186.

Mulvenon, James, and David Finkelstein, *China's Revolution in Doctrinal Affairs: Emerging Trends in the Operational Art of the Chinese People's Liberation Army*, Washington, D.C.: CNA Corporation, 2005.

Mulvenon, James C., and Andrew N. D. Yang, eds., *Seeking Truth from Facts: A Retrospective on Chinese Military Studies in the Post-Mao Era,* Santa Monica, Calif.: RAND Corporation, CF-160-CAPP, 2001. As of February 5, 2007: http://www.rand.org/pubs/conf_proceedings/CF160/

———, *A Poverty of Riches: New Challenges and Opportunities in PLA Research,* Santa Monica, Calif.: RAND Corporation, CF-189-NSRD, 2003.

Mulvenon, James C., and Richard H. Yang, eds., *The People's Liberation Army in the Information Age,* Santa Monica, Calif.: RAND Corporation, CF-145-CAPP/ AF, 1999. As of Febraury 5, 2007: http://www.rand.org/pubs/conf_proceedings/CF145/

Munson, Kenneth, "XAC JH-7," *Jane's All the World's Aircraft,* April 22, 2003.

———, "IAI Harpy and Cutlass," *Jane's Unmanned Aerial Vehicles and Targets,* February 20, 2004.

Nagy, Paul N., "Access is Key to Power Projection," *U.S. Naval Institute Proceedings,* Vol. 125, No. 2, February 1999.

National Defense Panel, *Transforming Defense: National Security in the 21st Century,* Arlington, Va., December 1997.

NDP—*See* National Defense Panel.

聶玉宝 [Nie Yubao], 〈打击海上敌大型舰艇编队的电子战战法〉 ["Electronic Warfare Methods for Striking Formations of Large Enemy Warships"], in Military Studies Editorial Department (1999).

Office of the Secretary of Defense, *Annual Report on the Military Power of the People's Republic of China,* Washington, D.C.: U.S. Department of Defense, May 2004. Online at http://www.defenselink.mil/pubs/d20040528PRC.pdf As of December 1, 2004).

———, *Annual Report to Congress: The Military Power of the People's Republic of China,* Washington, D.C.: U.S. Department of Defense, 2005. Online at http:// www.dod.mil/news/Jul2005/d20050719china.pdf As of February 6, 2006).

———, *Annual Report to Congress: Military Power of the People's Republic of China,* Washington, D.C.: U.S. Department of Defense, 2006. Online at http://www. dod.mil/pubs/pdfs/China%20Report%202006.pdf As of June 2, 2006).

O'Halloran, James C., "CNPMIEC FT-2000 Surface-to-Air Anti-Radiation Missile System," *Jane's Land-Based Air Defense,* August 17, 2004.

O'Malley, William D., *Evaluating Possible Airfield Deployment Options: Middle East Contingencies,* Santa Monica, Calif.: RAND Corporation, MR-1353-AF, 2001.

Onishi, Norimitsu, "Japan Support of Missile Shield Could Tilt Asia Power Balance," *New York Times,* April 3, 2004.

O'Rourke, Ronald, *China Naval Modernization: Implications for U.S. Navy Capabilities—Background and Issues for Congress*, November 18, 2005. As of January 25, 2006:
http://www.fas.org/man/crs/RL32665.pdf

"The Oscar Class: Organizing and Implementing Anti-Ship Operations," *Jianchuan Zhishi*, December 1, 2002, pp. 24–25. In Foreign Broadcast Information Service as "PRC: Tactics of Oscar-Class Submarine Anti-CVBG Warfare Detailed," December 1, 2002.

OSD—*See* Office of the Secretary of Defense.

Packard, Randall C., *The Unconventional Warfare Threat to the Afloat Prepositioning Force or How to Defeat a Marine Expeditionary Brigade If You Don't Have Any Tanks*, Newport, R.I.: Naval War College, 2000.

潘湘庭 [Pan Xiangting] and 孙占平 [Sun Zhanping], eds., 《高技术条件下美军局部战争》 [*The U.S. Military in Local Wars Under High-Technology Conditions*], Beijing: 解放军出版社 [Liberation Army Press], 1994.

Parsons, Ted, "China Develops Anti-Ship Missile," *Jane's Defence Weekly*, January 25, 2006.

彭光谦 [Peng Guangqian] and 姚有志 [Yao Youzhi], eds., 《战略学》 [*The Science of Strategy*], Beijing: 军事科学出版社 [Military Science Press], 2001.

Pillsbury, Michael, ed., *Chinese Views of Future Warfare*, Washington, D.C.: National Defense University Press, 1998.

Pillsbury, Michael, *China Debates the Future Security Environment*, Washington, D.C.: U.S. Government Printing Office, 2000.

Qu Xiaohua, Liu Zhanyong, and Shi Jun, 《出奇制胜:特种战》 [*Achieving Victory Through Surprise: Special Warfare*, Hebei: 河北科技出版社 [Science and Technology Press], 2000.

Ross, Robert S., "Navigating the Taiwan Strait: Deterrence, Escalation Dominance, and U.S.-China Relations," *International Security*, Vol. 27, No. 2, Fall 2002, pp. 48–85.

Rumsfeld, Donald H., *Quadrennial Defense Review Report*, Washington, D.C.: U.S. Department of Defense, September 2001.

———, *Transformation Planning Guidance*, Washington, D.C.: U.S. Department of Defense, April 2003. As of July 11, 2006:
http://www.oft.osd.mil/library/library_files/document_129_Transformation_Planning_Guidance_April_2003_1.pdf

Saunders, Stephen, "Han Class (Type 091) (SSN)," *Jane's Fighting Ships*, March 5, 2004a.

———, "Ming Class (Type 035) (SS)," *Jane's Fighting Ships*, March 5, 2004b.

————, "Romeo Class (Project 033) (SS)," *Jane's Fighting Ships*, March 5, 2004c.

————, "Song Class (Project 039) (SSG)," *Jane's Fighting Ships*, March 5, 2004d.

————, "Kilo Class (Project 877EKM/636) (SSK)," *Jane's Fighting Ships*, August 16, 2004e.

Sha Lin, "Two Senior Colonels and 'No-Limit Warfare,'" *Zhongguo Qingnian Bao*, June 28, 1999, p. 5. In Foreign Broadcast Information Service as "Two Senior Colonels on 'No-Limit Warfare,'" July 28, 1999.

Shambaugh, David, *Modernizing China's Military: Progress, Problems, and Prospects*, Berkeley, Calif.: University of California Press, 2002.

Shen Kuiguan, "Dialectics of Defeating the Superior with the Inferior," in Pillsbury (1998), pp. 218–219.

Shi Yukun, "Lt. Gen. Li Jijun Answers Questions on Nuclear Deterrence, Nation-State, and Information Age," *Zhongguo Junshi Kexue*, No. 3, August 20, 1995, pp. 70–76. In Foreign Broadcast Information Service as "General Li Jijun Answers Military Questions," August 20, 1995.

Shlapak, David A., John Stillion, Olga Oliker, and Tanya Charlick-Paley, *A Global Access Strategy for the U.S. Air Force*, Santa Monica, Calif.: RAND Corporation, MR-1216-AF, 2002. As of February 5, 2007: http://www.rand.org/pubs/monograph_reports/MR1216/

Shlapak, David A., and Alan Vick, *"Check Six Begins on the Ground": Responding to the Evolving Ground Threat to U.S. Air Force Bases*, Santa Monica, Calif.: RAND Corporation, MR-606-AF, 1995.

Siegel, Adam B., "Scuds Against Al Jubayl," *U.S. Naval Institute Proceedings*, Vol. 128, No. 12, December 2002.

Sirak, Michael, "US Vulnerable to EMP Attack," *Jane's Defence Weekly*, July 28, 2004.

Smith, Carroll J., David L. Cooksey, Frances W. Warren, and Edward F. O'Neill III, *Evaluation and Repair of War-Damaged Port Facilities, Report 2: Port Vulnerability, Pier and Wharf Repair and Storage Area Repair*, Washington, D.C.: U.S. Army Corps of Engineers, Technical Report GL-88-16, September 1988.

Smith, Roger, E. Anne Sandel, Gordon Nash, Mark Edwards, and Anthony Winns, "FY 2006 Navy Critical Systems Capabilities Programs," statement before the Subcommittee on Projection Forces of the House Armed Services Committee, March 15, 2005.

Stanton, Martin N., "Kamikazes, Q-Ships & Carrier Defense," *U.S. Naval Institute Proceedings*, Vol. 127, No. 12, December 2001.

Stillion, John, and David T. Orletsky, *Airbase Vulnerability to Conventional Cruise-Missile and Ballistic-Missile Attacks: Technology, Scenarios, and U.S. Air Force*

Responses, Santa Monica, Calif.: RAND Corporation, MR-1028-AF, 1999. As of February 5, 2007:
http://www.rand.org/pubs/monograph_reports/MR1028/

Stokes, Mark A., "The Chinese Joint Aerospace Campaign: Strategy, Doctrine, and Force Modernization," draft paper, October 2001.

孙利辉 [Sun Lihui], ed., 《海湾战争全史》 [*The Complete History of the Gulf War*], Beijing: 解放军出版社 [Liberation Army Press], 2002.

Sun Zian, "Strategies to Minimize High-Tech Edge of Enemy," *Xiandai Bingqi*, No. 8, August 8, 1995, pp. 10–11. In Foreign Broadcast Information Service as "Strategies Proposed to Minimize High-Tech Edge of Enemy," 1995.

Tang Baodong, "Difficulties in Pursuing Hegemony: Weakness of the United States in Fighting a Local War as Viewed from the Kosovo War," *Shanghai Guoji Zhanwang*, July 23, 1999. In Foreign Broadcast Information Service as "Commentary on 'Weakness' of US Hegemonism," August 23, 1999.

U.S. Air Force, *USAF Intelligence Targeting Guide*, Washington, D.C., Pamphlet 14-210 Intelligence, February 1, 1998. As of September 1, 2006:
http://www.fas.org/irp/doddir/usaf/afpam14-210/part00.htm

U.S. Department of Defense, *Background Briefing on the Defense Planning Guidance*, Washington, D.C., May 10, 2003. As of June 30, 2003:
http://www.defenselink.mil

———, *Dictionary of Military and Associated Terms*, Washington, D.C.: U.S. Government Printing Office, April 12, 2001 (as amended through October 7, 2004).

———, *The National Defense Strategy of the United States of America*, Washington, D.C., March 2005.

———, *Quadrennial Defense Review Report*, Washington, D.C., February 6, 2006.

U.S. Missile Defense Agency, "Aegis Ballistic Missile Defense (Aegis BMD)," fact sheet, July 2006. As of July 31, 2006:
http://www.mda.mil/mdalink/pdf/aegis.pdf As of July 31, 2006).

U.S. Navy, *Naval Transformation Roadmap: Power and Access . . . From the Sea*, Washington, D.C., March 4, 2003. As of July 31, 2006:
http://www.oft.osd.mil/library/library_files/document_202_naval_
transformation.pdf

"U.S. to Deploy Intercept Missiles in Japan," Associated Press, June 26, 2006.

Verschaeve, Pieter-Jan, "X-35 Joint Strike Fighter: Development Part 1," Web page, 2006. As of July 6, 2006:
http://www.topfighters.com/fighterplanes/jsf/development1.html

Vick, Alan, *Snakes in the Eagle's Nest: A History of Ground Attacks on Air Bases*, Santa Monica, Calif.: RAND Corporation, MR-553-AF, 1995. As of February 5, 2007:
http://www.rand.org/pubs/monograph_reports/MR553/

Vick, Alan, Richard Moore, Bruce Pirnie, and John Stillion, *Aerospace Operations Against Elusive Ground Targets*, Santa Monica, Calif.: RAND Corporation, MR-1398-AF, 2001. As of February 5, 2001:
http://www.rand.org/pubs/monograph_reports/MR1398/

王厚卿 [Wang Houqing] and 张兴业 [Zhang Xingye], eds., 《战役学》 [*Science of Campaigns*], Beijing: 国防大学出版社 [National Defense University Press], 2000.

Wang Hucheng, "The U.S. Military's Soft Ribs and Strategic Weaknesses," *Xinhua*, July 5, 2000. In Foreign Broadcast Information Service as "Liaowang on US Military's 'Strategic Weaknesses,'" July 5, 2000.

王沪鹰 [Wang Huying], 〈信息进攻的基本原则激战法〉 ["The Basic Principles and Campaign Methods of Information Attacks"], in Military Studies Editorial Department (1999).

Watanabe, Chisaki, "Japan, U.S. Announce Plan to Deploy Patriots in Okinawa," Associated Press, June 20, 2006.

Weaver, Greg, and J. David Glaes, *Inviting Disaster: How Weapons of Mass Destruction Undermine U.S. Strategy for Projecting Military Power*, McLean, Va.: AMCODA Press, 1997.

Wei Wei and Li Donghang, "Characteristics of U.S. Military Intervention Viewed in Reference to Kosovo War," *Jiefangjun Bao*, March 27, 2000. In Foreign Broadcast Information Service as "PLA Military Scholars on US Military Intervention," March 28, 2000.

魏岳江 [Wei Yuejiang], 〈我军探究新战法抗强敌远程超视距作战〉 ["Our Army Explores New Methods for Countering Enemy Over-the-Horizon Operations"], 《解放军报》 [*Liberation Army Daily*], January 27, 2003.

Wolthusen, Stephen D., "Self-Inflicted Vulnerabilities," *Naval War College Review*, Vol. LVII, Nos. 3–4, Summer–Autumn 2004, pp.103–113.

谢永高 [Xie Yonggao], 秦子增 [Qin Zizeng], and 黄海兵 [Huang Haibing], 〈军事航天技术的回顾与展望〉 ["Looking at the Past and Future of Military Aerospace Technology"], 《中国航天》 [*Aerospace China*], No. 6, 2002.

Xu Qi, "Russian Planes Play Around with the 'Small Eagle,'" *Jiefangjun Bao*, November 29, 2000. In Foreign Broadcast Information Service as "Russian Planes' Penetration of US Kitty Hawk's Defense Radar Network Viewed," November 29, 2000.

Xu Xiaoyan, "A Concept for a Strategy of Development in Which Informationization Drives Mechanization," *Zhongguo Junshi Kexue*, February 1,

2002. In Foreign Broadcast Information Service as "Chinese Military Official Outlines Strategy for Leaps of Technical Development," September 10, 2002.

徐源先 [Xu Yuanxian],〈试论未来我军信息战的基本样式〉["Future Basic Methods of Our Army's Information Warfare"], in Military Studies Editorial Department (1999).

Yang Guoliang, "National Security and the Building of 2nd Artillery Under New Historical Conditions," *Zhongguo Junshi Kexue*, November 11, 1998. In Foreign Broadcast Information Service as "PLA 2d Artillery Commander on Security," May 13, 1999.

Yang Yonghong, "The Latest Development of U.S. Supremacy," *Guoji Wenti Yanjiu*, October 13, 1999. In Foreign Broadcast Information Service as "Latest Developments in U.S. Hegemonism Noted," November 28, 1999.

Yi Jan, "Be Vigilant Over Japan's Future Role in the Taiwan Strait," *Ching Pao*, June 1, 2002. In Foreign Broadcast Information Service as "Ching Pao: 'Beijing Military Circles' Air Concern Over Japan's Future Role in Taiwan Strait," June 5, 2002.

展学习 [Zhan Xuexi], ed.,《战役学研究》[*Campaign Studies Research*], Beijing: 国防大学出版社 [National Defense University Press], 1997.

张建洪 [Zhang Jianhong],〈夺取战役制信息权作战探要〉["Operations to Achieve Campaign Information Control"], in Military Studies Editorial Department (1999).

Zhang Xianmin and Yi Ming, "Okinawa: How Much Longer Can the Star-Spangled Banner Flutter?" *Jiefangjun Bao*, July 26, 2000. In Foreign Broadcast Information Service as "PRC Paper Views US Military Bases on Okinawa," July 26, 2000.

Zhao Xijun, "'Victory Without War' and Modern Deterrence Strategy," *Zhongguo Junshi Kexue*, October 31, 2001, pp. 55–60. In Foreign Broadcast Information Service as "PRC Military Journal Explores Victory Without War, Modern Deterrence Strategy," December 28, 2001.

Zhou Jianguo and Xiao Wen, "A Breath-Taking Scene from the Sea of Japan: Russian Fighter Jets Conduct Sneak Attack on US Aircraft Carrier," *Jiefanjun Bao*, November 20, 2000. In Foreign Broadcast Information Service as "PRC Views Russian Jets Buzzing USS Kitty Hawk," November 20, 2000.

朱成虎 [Zhu Chenghu], Professor and Deputy Director of the Strategy Research Department, National Defense University,〈解决台湾问题不是实力问题,而是决心问题〉["Resolving the Taiwan Problem Is Not a Matter of Actual Strength, but a Matter of Determination"], interview, 2001. As of 2005: http://sis.ruc.edu.cn/daokan/200101/fangtan.html